CAPTAIN MAYNE REID

By JOAN STEELE

California State College, Stanislaus

TWAYNE PUBLISHERS

A DIVISION OF G. K. HALL & CO., BOSTON

823.8
R3575
1978

Library of Congress Cataloging in Publication Data

Steele, Joan.
  Captain Mayne Reid.

  (Twayne's English authors series ; 229)   Bibliography:
  p. 141 - 47
  Includes index.
  1.   Reid, Mayne, 1818 - 1883—Criticism and interpretation.
PR5219.R26Z93   823'.8   77-15975
ISBN 0-8057-6700-2

Twayne's English Authors Series

EDITOR OF THIS VOLUME

Herbert Sussman

Northeastern University

Captain Mayne Reid

TEAS 229

Captain Mayne Reid

For Mickey

Contents

About the Author

Joan Steele is the Senior Administrative Analyst at California State College, Stanislaus, with primary responsibility for affirmative action and coordination of academic research. She received her undergraduate and graduate education at the University of California, Los Angeles. Upon graduation with highest honors in English in 1961, she was elected to Phi Beta Kappa and was selected as a Woodrow Wilson Honorary Fellow for 1961 - 62. She was awarded the Ph.D. degree in 1970, with nineteenth-and twentieth-century English and American literature as her major fields. She has taught at Mount St. Mary's College; California State University, Los Angeles; and UCLA, and served as the coordinator of several federal educational grants at UCLA. In 1972 she received a grant from the American Philosophical Society to assist her in her research on *Captain Mayne Reid.*

Professor Steele has also published a bibliography on John Steinbeck and an article comparing Steinbeck's *Of Mice And Men* with Dickens's *Barnaby Rudge.*

Preface

In our age of mass communication, television and the paperback book cater to the entertainment of the masses. Today, as it has been ever since the discovery of the New World, the mass audience is thrilled by improbable tales of travel, science, danger, and adventure. This phenomenon did not come about at once; its origins may be found in the literary, theatrical, and journalistic productions of the past. Thus we may learn much from studying the works of an innovator in the field of popular literature: Captain Mayne Reid. In the mid-nineteenth century, his name was a household word—today he has faded into obscurity. The man, his work, and his audience are important not only as an historical curiosity, but also as a means of understanding the popular literature of our own time.

Mayne Reid was read by adults and children; he began his career writing fiction for adults based on his own experiences in the Western Hemisphere. Later he turned to writing adventure tales for boys that combined elements of Defoe and Cooper with his own unique passion for scientific accuracy. His aim was to present facts to English youth, and his method was to embroider his plots with excitement and natural history. So at first he wrote for two separate audiences. Later, when ill health restricted his activities and thus his range of subject matter, he began to adapt his "adult" romances for a juvenile audience by abridging them and republishing them as dime novels (the equivalent of today's comic book). So yet another generation of men and boys was introduced to the perils and charms of the prairies and mountains that Reid described with such gusto.

It is a measure of Reid's success in his own time that a writer such as Robert Louis Stevenson began his own attempts at fiction by imitating Reid, who was his favorite boyhood author. But unlike Stevenson, Reid was severely limited by the range of his imagination to tales based upon his own life experiences, and as the adventuresome part of his life spanned only his early years in America, he soon began to repeat himself. A reader familiar with the Reid canon can recognize plots and characters transposed from the vigorous works of the early fifties as they recur late in the seventies. This repetition represents a failure of imagination; it also results from the financial pressure common to writers of the period who ground out works to earn their livelihood by trying to satisfy an insatiable audience. These artistic limitations in Mayne Reid's works provide an unusual opportunity to observe how his use of autobiography and autobiographical fantasies appealed to the similar fantasies of a Victorian and post-Victorian public. One of the aims of this book is to explore these psychological ramifications.

Reid's work is particularly interesting in its variance from the norms of nineteenth-century popular fiction. Reid differs from most contemporary British writers, who were basically conservative in their politics and conventional in their treatment of women and exotic or oppressed peoples. Reid, however, was a radical republican who always espoused democratic if not anarchic principles. These appear when he depicts women who achieve an independent role in society and as he promotes the value of freedom for all races and nations—especially the oppressed. So a modern reader discerns, amid the stereotypes common to the tale of adventure, truly original characters struggling to break free from both the literary and social restrictions of the period. Because such a large percentage of Reid's audience was a youthful one, the commitment to these values of freedom was bound to influence their attitudes.

This book begins with a rather full account of Reid's biography, as a knowledge of any man is obviously essential to an understanding of his work. In Reid's case this is particularly important because so much of his work is autobiographical and all previously available biographical data has relied on his widow's inaccurate biographies—both long out of print.

Reid earned his reputation as a writer of fiction, and the focus of this book is on that genre. First his adult fiction is discussed according to its setting and themes. Then his juvenile fiction is examined and the relationship between the two is established. Finally, I have attempted to put into perspective this diverse canon: to go beneath the surface of hairbreadth escapes and peripatetic adventure to discover their deeper significance both to readers of the nineteenth century and to modern students seeking to understand the popular appeal of a writer who entered literature like a bursting rocket and then vanished with scarcely a trace in less than a hundred years.

JOAN STEELE

California State College,
Stanislaus

Acknowledgments

Initially, Professor Ada Nisbet encouraged me to explore this uncharted territory; all discoveries about Mayne Reid must therefore be credited to her. I am indebted to the American Philosophical Society, whose grant enabled me to travel to the United Kingdom and examine the Ollivant-Reid manuscripts and to discover that Elizabeth Reid's published biographies were in fact plagiarized from Charles Ollivant's manuscript. The search for those documents would have been fruitless had not Miss Alison Henry persuaded Mayne Reid's grandniece, Miss Poppy Mollan, to grant me permission to examine the material. I am more than grateful to Dr. E. Mayne Reid, C.B.E, F.R.I.C, and his wife, Meta Mayne Reid, of County Down. Their scholarly commitment through several years of transatlantic correspondence and their personal hospitality while I was in their troubled land made my work both rewarding and enjoyable. Finally, Michael Thomas Martin's able editorial assistance was instrumental in making this book a reality.

Chronology

1818   April 4. Thomas Mayne Reid born in Ballyroney, County Down, Northern Ireland.

1834   September. Enters Royal Academical Institution, Belfast.

1838   June. Leaves Royal Academical Institution and opens a small day school in a house near Ballyroney.

1839   December. Sails for New Orleans on *Dumfriesshire*. Reid's name does not appear on the passenger manifest.

1840   Employed by New Orleans corn-factor, leaving six months later after refusing to whip slaves. Travels to Nashville where he becomes tutor for the family of General Peyton Robertson. November 19—places advertisement in *Nashville Union* for December 1 opening of a "New English, Mathematical and Classical School."

1841   Becomes clerk for provision dealer in Natchitoches or Natchez, where he meets "Bill Garey," who persuades him to travel en route to the Pacific with a band of trappers. Meets Commodore Edwin W. Moore of the Texas Navy to whom he later dedicates *Scalp Hunters*.

1843   April. Travels west from St. Louis (according to various sources, either with Audubon to Fort Union or with Sir William Drummond Stewart to Wyoming). August—first poem published in *Godey's Magazine* under pseudonym "A Poor Scholar." Unsuccessful stint as an itinerant actor in Cincinnati. Autumn—meets Edgar Allan Poe in Philadelphia.

1846   December. Enlists in New York Volunteers to serve in Mexican War.

1847   January. Sails for Mexico. May 1—first "Sketches by a Skirmisher" published in *Spirit of the Times* under pseudonym "Ecolier." September 13—wounded at Battle of Chapultepec. September 16—promoted to first lieutenant.

1848   May. Mexico evacuated; Reid retires from army with rank of captain. October 23—*Love's Martyr* produced at the Walnut Street Theater for five performances.

1849   *War Life* privately printed in New York. June 27—sails for Liverpool with Friedrich Hecker and a band of volunteers formed to fight in the Bavarian revolution. July 12—returns to County Down for a month's visit, then settles in London.

1850   *The Rifle Rangers.*

1851   *The Scalp Hunters.* Meets Elizabeth Hyde, his future wife, then a child of thirteen.

1852   Visits France. Publishes *The Desert Home*, his first juvenile title.

1853   *The Boy Hunters*, Reid's first juvenile scientific travelog. Marries Elizabeth Hyde. Tries to smuggle the Hungarian revolutionary Louis Kossuth out of England.

1854   *Scalp Hunters* translated into French.

1855   *The White Chief.*

1856   *The Quadroon.* The Reids move to Gerrard's Cross, Buckinghamshire.

1859   *Oçeola.*

1860   *Odd People*, a collection of popularized anthropological studies of eighteen exotic tribes.

1861   November 18. Dion Boucicault's *Octoroon* presented at the Adelphi Theatre in London.

1863   November 26. Captain Reid addresses the American Thanksgiving Day dinner in London.

1864   April 29. "Garibaldi Rebuked" privately printed.

1865   *The Headless Horseman.*

1866   November 13. Reid declared bankrupt as a result of the construction of an elaborate reproduction of a Mexican hacienda, "The Ranche," and the failure of Overend, Gurney and Company.

1867   April 27 - May 22. Twenty-two issues of *The Little Times* appear in London. October—sails for America, settling in Newport, Rhode Island, in November.

1868   January. *The Helpless Hand*, Reid's first original Beadle and Adams Dime Novel. April—moves to New York. May—supposedly takes out United States naturalization papers. June—returns to England for a six-week visit to sell copyrights. July 11—*Headless Horseman* begins serial run in *Penny Miscellany*. October 14—Charles Ollivant sails for America to work with Reid as his private secretary.

CHAPTER 1

The Life of a Romantic Expatriate: A Writer's Profile

I The Quest for Adventure, 1818 - 1849

THOMAS Mayne Reid was born on April 4, 1818, to a family which had originated in Scotland and settled in Ballyroney, County Down, Northern Ireland, several generations before his birth. The Reid men traditionally had been called to the Presbyterian pulpit of that community; in June 1749, Mayne Reid's maternal great-grandfather, the Reverend Thomas Mayn, was ordained as minister of a congregation in Ballyroney, a post that he held for fifty-seven years. His grandson was the Reverend Thomas Mayne Reid, senior clerk of the Irish General Assembly and the father of Captain Mayne Reid. The ecclesiastical calling of the Reid men to the Presbyterian church stops at this point, for the rebellious, independent, and iconoclastic son turned first to adventures in the Americas and then to writing to establish his own fame.

Biographical data on Thomas Mayne Reid is scant and confusing. What we know about him during his early years is complicated by conflicting and ambiguous sources.[1] The present study makes use of the standard biographies of Reid's life and contemporary historical records, but especially Reid's extensive unpublished correspondence, which permits us to see Reid's life with greater clarity than before. However, the paucity of information, the contradictory accounts, and above all the confused and circuitous relationship between Reid's fiction and his life make the biography a tortuous and nearly impossible puzzle to solve.

We know so little about Reid's childhood and youth up until the time he left for America that even conjectural statements about the early formative influences on his life are not possible. The Reverend Thomas Mayne Reid, Captain Mayne Reid's father, intended for his son to follow him into the ministry, and sent him to the Royal

Academical Institution in Belfast at the age of sixteen for that purpose, although it is doubtful that he completed the prescribed course. A more unlikely candidate for the ministry can scarcely be imagined. Reid was a wild youth who had little interest in a classical education, generally preferring to roam the Mourne Hills pursuing game or observing nature. It is not surprising that he abandoned his studies at the Royal Academical Institution without completing them.

According to all accounts, Reid—a restless youth driven by wanderlust and a desire for grand adventures—persuaded his parents to release him from his studies and to let him make his way in the New World. With their consent, he sailed for New Orleans in December 1839. Having thrown his letters of introduction overboard in a pique after discovering that several of his fellow passengers had similar letters, Reid began his American career entirely on his own. The absence of factual detail about Reid's life (particularly his early adventures in the United States) is not surprising, for as one of many young unknown adventurers roaming the trans-Mississippi West at that time, he was not likely to be noticed. Thus the first several years of Reid's career are difficult to trace; what follows is as accurate a reconstruction as the sources and the correspondence permit.

In New Orleans Reid obtained a situation with a large commission house where among other duties he had charge of slave gangs. He left that employment after an incident in which he refused to whip the slaves. In the early autumn of 1840, Reid went to Nashville, Tennessee, where he became a tutor in the home of General Peyton Robertson. Reid's career as a schoolmaster can be traced from a series of advertisements in the pages of the *Nashville Union* promoting his "New English, Mathematical and Classical School." The first ad appeared in the issue of November 19, 1840, and ran weekly through January 1841. The ad read in part:

Instructions will be given in the following subjects:
Mathematics, viz: Elements of Geometry, Plain and Spherical Trigonometry, Algebra, Mensuration, Surveying, and Arithmetic, &c.
Natural Philosophy, viz: Laws of Motion, Mechanics, Hydrostatics, Hydraulics and Astronomy.
English Grammar, Geography, History, English Reading, Writing and Elocution.
Classics, viz: Greek, Latin and Hebrew. . . . I am a graduate of the

Royal College, Belfast, Ireland, and my degree qualifies me to teach any of the above mentioned branches.

As far as we know Reid's claim to be a graduate of the "Royal College" is suspect. Perhaps the incredible range of courses listed above was more than the twenty-two-year-old Reid could handle. Whatever the reasons, Reid's next advertisement shows a marked change in the curriculum, shifting the school's emphasis toward the more utilitarian branches of learning: "Feeling convinced, from experience, of the absolute inutility of the Classical studies, though compelled by the trammels of custom and hoary usage, and by respect due to the authority of others, to acknowledge them as branches of Education, I will nevertheless consider them as holding a secondary rank in my school. . . . English education [i.e., correct reading, writing, and speaking] . . . Studies of Geography and History . . . the Mathematical and Philosophical sciences, with their practical application to the useful arts of life will form the primary elements of my school." This second notice ran from March 1, 1841, through June 14, 1841.

On July 1, the schoolmaster announced a much-requested holiday, but after this no more was heard of the "English, Classical and Mathematical School" or its pedagogue. Mrs. Reid states that her husband drew on his Tennessee experiences for the novel *Wild Huntress* (1861), but it must have been only for the setting, for the schoolmaster in that novel is an archvillain, and the novel's autobiographical character, Edward Warfield, has just returned from the Mexican War, which would make any biographical linkage to Reid's Tennessee experiences of 1840 - 41 anachronistic.

Following a brief stint as a store clerk in either Natchez, Mississippi, or Natchitoches, Louisiana, Reid supposedly went on two extensive trading expeditions with the Indians along the Red River. One of these trips, from St. Louis to Santa Fe and then to Chihuahua, probably was the basis for parts of *The Desert Home* (1852) and certainly for much of *Scalp Hunters* (1851). According to Mrs. Reid, the young former schoolteacher began organizing game-hunting expeditions, and "on one of these, starting from St. Louis, he was accompanied, among others, by Audubon, the famous naturalist, who took an especial interest in giving Mayne Reid the benefit of his experience."[2] Audubon led an expedition up the Missouri River from St. Louis to Ft. Union on the Montana - North

Dakota border in April 1843. This party was composed of over a hundred persons (mostly French and Canadian trappers), to assist Audubon in compiling material for his projected *Quadrupeds of North America*. And although Reid would have been interested in the scientific aspect of such a journey, he would not have liked the confinement of shipboard life.

Reid probably would have been even more interested in travelling overland with the hunting party of Sir William Drummond Stewart. Stewart, the most famous of many aristocratic British travellers in the Far West, was out for pure adventure. He was in St. Louis at the same time as Audubon, preparing for a trek very similar in its adventures to those of the physician, the naturalists, and the British nobleman seeking buffalo and discoveries in natural history described in Reid's *The Hunter's Feast* (1856). Stewart's more daring expedition might have been more to Reid's taste. However, it is not possible to relate the biography to the novel with any precision. The same holds true for most of Reid's novels. Mrs. Reid, when describing her husband's experiences in America, is annoyingly vague and circuitous: her supposedly factual biographies often depend upon Reid's novels, which themselves are often little more than a thinly disguised biography mixed with fanciful experiences which Reid presented as factual. Thus it is impossible to verify his whereabouts during these early years.

Reid probably arrived in Philadelphia in the autumn of 1843, for that is where he first met Edgar Allan Poe, who moved to New York on April 6, 1844. The extent of the Reid-Poe friendship is uncertain, but that Reid knew Poe is evident from the recollections of Thomas Cottrell Clarke's nephew, Howard Paul, who was present at some of the monthly dinner parties in Clarke's home that Poe and Reid attended. Paul's description of Reid at these gatherings is of especial interest, as it gives us one of a very few portraits of the young author in America:

One of his [Poe's] intimates was Captain Mayne Reid, and when these two forgathered, as they frequently did, at my uncle's table, they would exchange opinions and argue in the most brilliant manner. . . . Mayne Reid was a fluent, inexhaustible *raconteur*, and shone to advantage when relating his adventures of travel. . . . Poe was of the opinion that Mayne Reid had an exuberantly inventive imagination when he talked of his own exploits, and I heard him assure my uncle, one evening, that Reid was "a collossal but most picturesque liar. He fibs on a surprising scale," he added, "but with the finish of an artist, and that is why I listen to him attentively."

Paul also remembers hearing Reid "relate with circumstantial detail that he had 'just been out West fighting Indians,' when I happened to know that he had been boarding quietly at a farm house in New Jersey."[3]

While in his essay, "A Dead Man Defended" *(Onward,* 1 [April 1869], 305 - 08) Reid claims to have known Poe for two years, conflicting evidence (such as descriptions and dates of Poe's residences) suggests that this is impossible. Perhaps Reid allowed his lively imagination to embellish his acquaintance with Poe, and later biographers have simply taken him at his word.

Reid probably remained in Philadelphia during the years 1844 - 46, and published a number of poems and tales in *Godey's* and in *Graham's Magazine.* While Elizabeth Reid says that he completed his five-act tragedy, *Love's Martyr,* in Philadelphia on November 20, 1846, she also states that he left Philadelphia in the spring of that year, spending the summer at Newport, Rhode Island, "as correspondent to the *New York Herald* under the name of 'Ecolier.' " So once again it is impossible to verify Reid's whereabouts during these early years in America.

Reid's early poems published in *Godey's* and *Graham's* magazines are of slight interest. They are generally short and deal with unrequited love and the beauties of nature—matters of some concern to their young author—while occasional foreshadowings of the narratives of later years also occur. For example, "My Star-Browed Steed: A Mexican Patriot's Lament," could easily have been written by the heroine of *War Trail,* grieving for the loss of her mount. "La Cubana," a fragment appearing in *Godey's* from February through May of 1845, itself plagiarizes whole lines from Reid's earlier poem, "Tropic Land." And the six columns of "Scouting Near Vera Cruz," in *Graham's* (33 [October 1848], 211 - 13), are an intermediate draft of the "bathing incident" in *War Life* and *Rifle Rangers.*

Reid's play *Love's Martyr* represents his earliest efforts in the drama. The play is a melodrama redolent with echoes of Byron's verse and *Othello's* plot, set in the Venice of 1400. The plot concerns the Venetian general Casimir, whose young wife Marinella is secretly in love with her brother Basil. The Iagolike villain Caraffa plants suspicions in Casimir's mind, but the hero, a man of strong republican sentiments and high morality, overhears the young pair forswearing their passion because of the honor and duty that they owe him; Casimir promptly forgets all thoughts of vengeance.

Shortly thereafter he is mortally wounded defending Florence against the Milanese, and gives his deathbed blessing to Marinella and Basil (who, it turns out, are not really siblings). The play was not reviewed by the Philadelphia press, but Reid's concern for preserving it is apparent; he had it privately printed in 1849. This early interest in the drama was to revive in later years and represents a significant variation in his career, although most of his scripts were never printed and therefore remain unknown to all but a few scholars.

Reid was mustered into the First New York Volunteer Regiment as a second lieutenant on December 3, 1846, and sailed for Vera Cruz the following January. Now at last Lieutenant Reid becomes visible, for Reid had accepted a post as a war correspondent for the newspaper *Spirit of the Times*. Reid's first contribution appears in the edition of May 1, 1847, under the caption, " 'Sketches by a Skirmisher' Written for *Spirit of the Times* by an Officer of the United States Army," and signed "Ecolier" (17 [May 1, 1847], 109 - 11). The "Sketches" continued their *Spirit of the Times* run through December 18, 1847.[4] Reid was recognized for his personal heroism, which merited mention from his superior officers, though the exact nature and importance of Reid's role in the campaign was a subject of dispute.

Reid was cited for his bravery at the battle of Chapultepec. He sustained a severe thigh wound in the battle which was to plague him for the rest of his life. On September 16, 1847, while hospitalized, he was promoted to first lieutenant. Controversy later arose over the matter of Reid's heroism at Chapultepec. While Reid himself never claimed to have been "first" or to have raised the flag over the fortress, some accounts do credit him with that distinction. Reid apparently was obsessed with clarifying his involvement and importance in this battle; to this end he collected testimonies from his comrades before he left America in 1849. Many of these testimonies are printed in Mrs. Reid's biographies. In the last years of his life, more than thirty years later, Reid was still engaged in transatlantic correspondence regarding his brief military career.

While convalescing from his battle wound, Reid began to investigate the charms of Mexican society. He was attracted to those members of the aristocracy that were sympathetic to the American cause, and was particularly enchanted by their young women. Here he evidently acquired his taste for the dark, even slightly mustachioed, ladies who appear so often in his novels. Eventually, conflicting rumors reached the eastern United States and Reid's family in Northern Ireland: that he had been killed in the battle, and that he was "about to be married to Signorina Gaudaloupe [sic] Rozas, a beautiful lady, and said to be the wealthiest heiress in the Valley of Mexico" (pp. 70 - 77). Both reports seem to be examples of what Howard Paul described as Reid's "exuberantly inventive imagination as to his own exploits."

In the face of Reid's silence, his family believed him dead. He did not write to his father until January 20 of the following year, determined not to communicate with his family until he had taken "rank among men—to prove myself not unworthy of that gentle blood from which I am sprung." This letter reveals a paradoxical side of Reid's nature: proud throughout his career of his republican, antiaristocratic ideals, he nevertheless retained a number of aristocratic pretentions. This paradox may in part explain the lack of consistency characteristic of both his life and work.

In May 1848 Mexico was evacuated, and Reid resigned from the army with the rank of captain, by which title he would be known for the rest of his life. Once again he enters a period of relative obscurity. Mrs. Reid reports that he spent the summer and autumn in Newport and Philadelphia, writing for various journals, while other sources state that he spent the autumn and winter of 1848 - 49 with his friend and fellow journalist Donn Piatt in Ohio. Reid completed his first successful work, *The Rifle Rangers* (1850), at the Piatt home.

Reid apparently returned to New York in the spring of 1849, but there is no trace of his activities for the remainder of his stay in America, other than Mrs. Reid's claim that he was "an interested participator" in demonstrations supporting European revolutionary movements then occurring in New York City. Reid sailed for England on June 27 in the company of a band of volunteers for the purpose of aiding the Bavarian revolutionists (pp. 93, 97).

II *The Hero Returns to England, 1849 - 1867*

Mayne Reid, the thirty-one-year-old former captain from the Mexican-American War, returned to England on July 10, 1849. For the next eighteen years Reid lived in England, where he occasionally involved himself in various revolutionary causes and political issues. These years witnessed the rise of Reid's literary career to its height as the captain produced a steady stream of novels and "Boys'

Books." But these were also years of financial extravagance, as Reid indulged his taste in clothes, liquor, and architecture—eventually to the point of bankruptcy. By 1867 Reid's career was declining, and he returned to America, the land of his early adventure and success, to try his hand once more.

When Reid returned to England in the summer of 1849, the Bavarian revolution for which he was headed had already come to an end. After taking time for a month's reunion with his family, Reid rejoined his men to go to Hungary to fight in the republican cause; however, despite the claims made by Mrs. Reid, there is no record of Reid's active involvement in this revolution.

Reid now settled down to establish his career as an author. He found an English publisher for *Rifle Rangers* and with that his literary career was launched. Following his American pattern, Reid sent poetry to *Bentley's Miscellany*, but to no avail, as no verse by Reid appears in the magazine for 1849 or 1850. However, when *Rifle Rangers* was published by Shoberl in the spring of 1850, it received a favorable review in the *Miscellany:* "He has given us a work which contains all the interest of a striking romance. . . . There are some nice descriptions of Mexican scenery, dashed off with a free hand, and the peculiarities in the character, costumes and customs of the natives, are well delineated. . . . Captain Reid is a fine manly 'go-ahead' fellow who will be sure to win his way to the good opinion and regard of the reader" (23 [1850] 220). It is significant that the reviewer should have chosen the nineteenth-century adjective "go-ahead" to describe Reid, for this epithet described the bustle and progress of the new American industrialization—an American quality not stressed in Reid's works.

Reid went to his family home at Mourne View, Ballyroney, sometime in 1850 to write his next novel, *The Scalp Hunters*, based in part on his adventures with the Santa Fe traders. He returned to London with the manuscript, which was published by Skeet in 1851, and remained in the city for the next several years, writing and busying himself in political causes of various kinds. In 1851 Reid met his future wife, Elizabeth Hyde, then a child of thirteen who later recalled sewing dolls' clothes at their first meeting. Inquiring her age, the dashing captain said, "You are getting old enough to have a lover, and you must have me!" whereupon he gave her a copy of *Scalp Hunters*. On first seeing Elizabeth, Reid had exclaimed to himself, "this is Zöe," she reminded him so much of his own fictional adolescent heroine.

The match between the thirty-three-year-old author and the thirteen-year-old girl was certainly worthy of one of Reid's own novels and evokes an inevitable comparison with Poe and his child-wife, Virginia, for whom Reid expressed great admiration. Reid married Elizabeth Hyde two years after their first meeting. Presumably the marriage took place during the summer, for by the hunting season the newlyweds were spending their time at Stokenchurch, Oxfordshire. Elizabeth was the only daughter of George William Hyde, a granddaughter of Saville John Hyde, and a lineal descendant of Edward Hyde, the first Earl of Clarendon. If the autobiographical parts of Reid's novel *The Child Wife* (1868) are to be trusted, Miss Hyde's aristocratic father looked with great disfavor on this match—as well he might, considering its incongruity. Reid was a man of experience, a soldier, and a radical, and Elizabeth's position in English society had not prepared her for marriage to the flamboyant and politically "unstable" author. She was often discontented, especially during the time they spent in the United States.

During this period Reid was writing furiously. He produced three-decker novels (those handsomely bound three-volume affairs that graced Victorian bookshelves) based on his real or imaginary adventures in America. He also discovered a talent—and a market—for "Boys' Books"—full of the excitement of the hunt in distant lands with copious descriptions of nature designed to improve the minds of young readers. In 1852, the first of these books, *The Desert Home*, was published in London by David Bogue. This was perhaps the best in a long line of books written for British and American youths. Reid wrote nearly as many of these boys' books as he did adult books, and although he enjoyed immense popularity and even adulation from his youthful audience, he later regretted his effort in this field, feeling that it detracted from his literary stature.

In 1853 Reid was active in Hungarian politics on behalf of the patriot and revolutionary Louis Kossuth. Several unpublished letters to Charles Kent of the *London Sun* confirm Reid's interest in the Hungarian cause. Mrs. Reid also writes of her husband's plan to smuggle Kossuth out of England disguised as his servant. Reid later fictionalized some of the details of the Kossuth affair in *The Child Wife* (1868).

After 1853 Reid's correspondence reveals the first hint of one of the problems he was to encounter throughout the rest of his professional life—the charge of plagiarism. On October 10, 1854, Reid defended himself against such a suggestion. Attempting to find a German publisher for *Rifle Rangers* and *Scalp Hunters*, Reid wrote to Nicholas Trübner: "You state that my writings very much resemble those of Sealsfield. I cannot tell whether or no, as I am but very little acquainted with the works of that author. I have heard that they are very popular in Germany. From what I know of the German people, I am led to believe that works of adventure such as mine are would be more welcome to them than the usual fashionable novels." Reid also sought a continental market in France; both *Scalp Hunters* and *The White Chief* appeared in French between 1854 and 1861, testifying to Reid's early popularity in France.

In the autumn of 1856, the Reids moved to Gerrard's Cross, Buckinghamshire, where much of his later work was written. Here Reid built a home in the style of a Mexican hacienda, even calling it "The Ranche." Reid was his own architect, and his insistence on authenticity extended to supervising the brickmaking himself; the bricks were made (in the "Mexican style") on the property. Such attention to detail contributed to the financial difficulties reflected in Reid's frequent harassment of publishers on both sides of the Channel and the Atlantic. His correspondence also reveals a concern for his reputation as an author of quality work. On June 6, 1859, he wrote to the American publishers Ticknor and Fields that "there are houses in your country who are willing to give £100 for a novel of my writing—therefore *you must do the same. . . .* You need not fear the *quality* of the work. Have confidence therefore in me and if you wish to express that confidence in a substantial form send on one of those pretty sybilline [sic] leaves addressed to Messrs. Baring!"

Reid was immensely active during this period, not only in writing novels and negotiating for their publication, but in producing nonfiction and adapting his novels for the stage. On April 1, 1865, Reid's play *The Maroon* was produced at the Royal Victoria Theatre for an indeterminate run. In the nineteenth century a play could not be produced on the London stage without prior licensing by the Lord Chamberlain. This censorship proceeding has preserved many manuscripts that otherwise would have been lost. Thus the manuscript of *The Maroon* provides the only firm evidence both of Reid's authorship and its production. The *Maroon* script appears in the *Lord Chamberlain's Daybooks* as five quarto manuscript folders written in various hands. Acts 3-5 and the Prologue seem to have been transcribed by Elizabeth Reid.

Reid's fiction also was popular as a foundation for other dramatists. As early as 1853, *Seguin the Scalp Hunter* was licensed for production at the City of London Theatre. The manuscript (which includes the censor's instruction to "omit all oaths and 'by Jasus' in representation") reveals the work to be a three-act adaptation of Reid's novel, faithful to the original plot and characters (*Lord Chamberlain's Daybooks*, II [1852 - 65], p. 252). And the spectacular elements that characterized Reid's work appeared to attract an unknown adapter for Astley's Amphitheatre, who lifted *War Trail*, lock, stock, and Moro (the hero's horse), for presentation there as "a grand Mexican equestrian spectacle in three acts" for presentation on October 18, 1857 (British Museum MS. 474.e9, Vol. 5 [1857], p. 212).

A drama entitled *Oçeola* (containing only the melodramatic plot without the historical detail of Reid's novel) was produced at the Surrey Theatre on April 19, 1859, while C. H. Hazlewood's version of Reid's *Headless Horseman* (1865) was performed at the Brittania Theatre as *The Headless Horseman; or The Ride of Death* that same year. Hazlewood acknowledged that the play was adapted from Reid's novel, unlike Dion Boucicault, who plagiarized Reid's 1856 novel *The Quadroon* for his play *The Octoroon*, which was produced at the Adelphi Theatre in London on November 18, 1861, following its first appearance on December 16, 1859, at the Winter Garden in New York.

Dion Boucicault's plagiarized drama threw Reid into a frantic state, and he began a lengthy correspondence in the pages of the *Athenaeum*, attacking Boucicault for appropriating his novel. Apparently Reid was particularly incensed by Boucicault's changing the title to "Octoroon," which he insisted was not an accurate word for the racial mixture it represents. Indeed, the first appearance of "octoroon" in the *Oxford English Dictionary* is as the title of Boucicault's play; it is an interesting sidelight on Reid's character that he should be so infuriated by an etymological detail.

Reid was never very successful in his theatrical ventures. In a letter to Charles Ollivant, May 21, 1879, Reid reminisced about the failure of his adaptation of *The Maroon:* "it was too carelessly put up, and did not succeed by reason of the bad actors they had there." Reid had dramatized the novel as a vehicle for George Jamison, the famous American actor. If the play featured Jamison, a seasoned performer, Reid's complaint is perhaps an example of his tendency to abrogate the responsibility for his own failures.

Reid's interest in the drama extended throughout his career. We recall that he had a brief career as an actor during his first stay in America, and that his five-act tragedy *Love's Martyr* was produced in Philadelphia in 1848. Thus, as his career began to ebb toward the very end of his life, it is hardly surprising that he would consider the stage once more. In 1874, Reid corresponded with P. T. Barnum; he proposed writing a drama based on Livingstone and tried to interest Barnum in staging an adaptation of *Wild Huntress*, but the plans were never realized and the combination of Mayne Reid and P. T. Barnum never reached the footlights.

At the end of 1862, one of the more mysterious events of Reid's life and literary career began to unfold. According to Mrs. Reid's account, a stranger named Charles Beach presented himself at the Reid's London house clad in a kind of *serape*, so far removed from civilization that he did not remember how to use a knife and fork. This curious figure "carried a brown paper parcel under his arm. Mayne Reid listened to his story, which was to the effect that he had lately landed from Australia, and that he had travelled around the earth more than six times, and had also lived with cannibals" (p. 149). Duly christened "Cannibal Charlie" by his host, Charles Beach left the brown paper parcel with Reid for his revisions of the manuscript it contained; this eventually resulted in the publication in 1864 of *Lost Lenore: or The Adventures of a Rolling Stone.* The catalogue of the British Museum lists "Charles Beach" as a pseudonym for Mayne Reid, and despite Mrs. Reid's testimony, it would be tempting to conclude that the entire Cannibal Charlie story was manufactured by the captain himself. But there are extreme stylistic differences between the two authors. Beach's works read very much like Horatio Alger transplanted to far-off places. The rapid pace of the story line allows for none of the nature description common in Reid's work; the mysteries are never solved (not even in three concluding paragraphs, as is Reid's practice), and the works are weakened by extensive use of the passive voice not characteristic of Reid.

The fragmentary evidence suggests that *Lost Lenore* and six other "Beach" novels, although having been accepted as products of Reid's pen, are in reality the work of some other writer, though not necessarily the person described in Mrs. Reid's biography. They may be plagiarisms or translations from a foreign author, for Reid, in spite of his attitude of shocked outrage toward Boucicault, was guilty of both.

During the sixties Reid had attained sufficient fame to be the subject of two parodies. The first appeared in *Fun* (1863), which had Reid, along with such other Victorian "greats" as Thackeray, Trollope, Dickens, and Collins forming the "London Joint-Stock Novel Company," in order to produce the composite novel "Philip Dombey, The Scalp-Hunter's Roundabout Secret Legacy." Capturing the captain's character quite well, *Fun* reports that Reid "has kindly insisted on writing the first chapter."[5]

The second parody was even more devastating. "The Skull Hunters," the first of a series projected by *Judy*, appeared in the issue of May 22, 1867. The title page states: "Capt. Rayne Meade also authored the Prairie Pumpkin, The Indian Thief, 'Possum Chief, Kitchen Rangers, Mouse Trappers, The War Whoop of the Ojabberways, Humbug of the Rocky Mts., Mosquito Hunters, Flea Hunters, Holman Hunters, etc." In his generous use of alliteration, juxtaposition of zoological and geographical impossibilities, apostrophe and hyperbole, the parodist captured his subject to perfrction in such passages as: "Land of Anahuac! Region of Montezuma! How often on my Brazilian barb have I bounded over thy boundless snow-capped prairies and grass-grown mountains in pursuit of possums, hyenas, boa-constrictors, and polar bears!" (p. 11). While these parodies do not flatter Reid, they indicate just how much of a household word his name and style had become during these years.

Reid's interests extended beyond his own literary career and the European revolutions. Always a defender of oppressed peoples, Reid involved himself in the issues of the American Civil War. In a letter to Ticknor he stated that "Those fools in Carolina are going mad. If they were free from the Northern Union for ten years their own blacks would eat them up and in truth that is likely to be the end of their bragging history. Carolina should be allowed to try it I think." Mrs. Reid reports that her husband believed strongly in the Union, which is amply demonstrated by the closing quatrain of his 1861 poem, "To the United States":

> Woe, woe to the world, if this fatal division
> Should ever arrive in the ranks of the free!
> Oh, brother! Avoid then the deadly collision,
> And millions unborn will sing praises to thee!
>
> (p. 147)

By 1863 Reid had attained sufficient reputation as both author and soldier to be asked to speak in response to the toast to the army and navy at the American Thanksgiving Day dinner held at St. James's Hall, London, on November 26. Reid was in the distinguished company of Charles Francis Adams and other members of the American legation. His remarks tended toward hyperbole, but they indicated where his honest sympathies lay, and his speech was greeted with loud cheers from everyone present. Speaking on behalf of the Union cause, Reid said, "I am half an American in nationality [sic] and wholly one in heart. . . . I feel something of shame that my sword has not gone with my soul into that struggle between God and the devil upon the other side of the Atlantic which is now progressing." Reid went on to affirm the rightness of the Union's cause and to compare the issue of American slavery with the tyranny of the English Establishment. In fact he dared, on English soil, to make one cause complement the other: "It is perfectly absurd to suppose that the half dozen lordlings, who, under the pseudonym of statesmen, preside over the destinies of England, can scarcely be ignorant of the terrible legacy that they are leaving to England's people. They may not live to see it administered, though it will some day yet be distributed in tears. What care they! Statesmen, forsooth! . . . expounders of fossilized formularies, which have so long held the whole of the human race in thraldom."[6]

At this time Reid became interested in Garibaldi as an apostle of freedom, and corresponded with Maltus Questell Holyoake in hopes of obtaining an introduction to the Italian revolutionary. Holyoake, an ardent young admirer of Reid's work, arranged the meeting, but Reid then rather quixotically declined the honor on the grounds that Garibaldi had been corrupted by the English Establishment. Garibaldi's remarks in a speech at the Crystal Palace praising English freedom—especially freedom of speech—had offended Reid, who believed such freedom in England to be tenuous at best. Garibaldi's admiration of England struck Reid as sycophantic and it alienated him. As touchy in politics as in literature, and sensitive to slights—real or imagined—Reid was easily alienated. His political enemies ranged from Palmerston and Gladstone to Disraeli; his letters are full of diatribes attacking whoever was in political power. Thus it is tempting to see Mayne Reid as an anarchic rebel whose sympathies lay always with the outsider striving for power. That power, once attained, made its holder an insider, part of the

Establishment and hence anathema to Reid. This is reinforced by a number of his works in which political figures appear; the early short story "The Death of Cordova" shows Simón Bolívar as tyrant rather than liberator, and *The Tiger Hunter* demolishes the myth of Morelos as a leader in the fight for Mexican independence.

As the sixties wore on, Reid's political involvements and increased literary output did little to rescue him from incipient bankruptcy. Although Elizabeth Reid claims great financial success for the publications, her husband was a notorious spendthrift; his wardrobe alone would bankrupt an ordinary man. His sartorial elegance verged on dandyism—but with unusual touches of eccentricity. Many a Victorian fancied yellow gloves and fine boots, but few would parade on the local common in a Norfolk jacket and Mexican sombrero. He bought on impulse, yet was meticulous in his details, even to the precise specifications of the shirtstuds and haberdashery trimmings he ordered. In addition to such personal extravagance, "The Ranche" at Gerrard's Cross also proved to be a financial disaster. When his bank failed on November 13, 1866, Reid was bankrupt.

Reid worked tirelessly to pay off his bankruptcy obligations, and was fortunate in his admirers. One of his youthful readers had been Charles Ollivant; the young man from Manchester had read all of Reid's work, and worshipped the author from afar. One day in August 1865 he summoned his courage and wrote to his hero: "Dear Captain: I feel that I have the right to address you thus, as one of your ardent boy-readers. If I do not know you personally I have been acquainted with you for ten years through your delightful books. Words fail to express my admiration for them. Ah! Captain, I shudder to think how I might have been floundering in the mires of *Toryism* and king-worship, but for the pure teachings and love of Republican liberty enculcated in your writings." Ollivant continued, expressing his desire to abandon his family's commercial business, to become a writer, and to become Mayne Reid's private secretary.

Reid's friendly reply, addressed to "Master" Charles Ollivant, was gracious and kind. Although he could not offer Ollivant a position because of his present financial condition, his courteous response so encouraged Charles that their relationship soon became permanent. After several months of correspondence, Charles began to prove the depths of his loyalty, which was both personal and enduring. On his own initiative, Ollivant organized a committee to help Reid out of his financial difficulties. The committee placed an ad in the London *Times* on November 30, 1866, requesting every reader who had ever enjoyed a Mayne Reid work to purchase a copy of his latest book, *The Headless Horseman*. Thus Ollivant's efforts saved Reid from total financial collapse.

Mayne Reid's letters to Charles Ollivant are perhaps his most honest exposure of self; they contain fragments of truth he would not have trusted to anyone else. And from this correspondence occasionally arise mildly shocking tidbits of literary and personal gossip: the news that he had paid someone in America "a good deal of money" for "rough writing" *The White Squaw;* his offer to provincial papers in 1879 of Frederick Whittaker's *The Cadet Button* as his own work (only to have it rejected by all the editors); his delight at being accepted by country aristocracy (despite all his protestations of equality and republicanism).

Reid's literary judgment resembled his political enthusiasms and financial extravagances: all were impetuous. After his discharge from bankruptcy on January 10, 1867, he embarked on a venture that would have been risky at best but was irrational indeed for a man in his circumstances: the establishment of a new penny evening journal, the *Little Times,* of which he was the sole proprietor and editor. It is hard to imagine what strange whim caused Reid to imitate his old Tory enemy the London *Times,* but the venture failed after twenty-two issues. It may be found today only in one bound copy in the Newspaper Library of the British Museum. Once the property of the faithful Charles Ollivant, and with a table of contents painstakingly transcribed in Ollivant's own hand, this volume is the only remaining trace of Reid's prodigious labor.

At the end of his financial resources in England, Reid fortunately was still in demand in America, particularly to write "dime novels" for the famous publisher Beadle and Adams. It is not surprising that at forty-nine, with his career seriously waning in England, he should decide to return to the land of his youthful adventures, hoping to recapture some of his earlier glory, rebuild his finances, and improve his literary reputation. In October 1867 the Reids sailed for America.

III   *A Fresh Start in America, 1867 - 1870*

Reid's second sojourn in the United States was much shorter than his first. The middle-aged author returned to America seeking not adventure but financial success. His three-year stay was character-ized by feverish efforts to revive his literary career, production of the short-lived periodical *Onward,* and domestic difficulties stem-ming from his wife's dislike for America. At the end of this period, Reid departed the land of his early adventures for a final time, a sick man on the verge of both mental and physical collapse.

After their arrival in New York in October, the Reids moved to Newport, Rhode Island, on November 8, 1867. The captain began to write novels once more and to engage in extensive cor-respondence about his serial and other publications. A letter to the editor of the *Fireside Companion* from this period tells us of his ac-tivities and concern over his newest effort, *Finger of Fate.* Reid wrote the novel in 1867, just after the collapse of the *Little Times.* The first installment appeared in the *Boys' Own Magazine* in December 1867. Mrs. Reid reports that "the proprietor of the *Fireside Companion,* New York, paid the sum of $5,000 for the right to run this romance in his paper" (p. 172).

Reid's correspondence about this time contains many complaints about the pirating of his novels by the American publisher Robert M. De Witt. De Witt also attempted to capitalize on Reid's fame by attributing to him several titles that he did not write. In a letter to Harper Bros. dated February 1, 1868: Reid charges that "Dewitt [sic] of your city . . . has not only taken them [Reid's novels] without a word to me, but has also committed himself by publishing under my name several volumes I have not written." Reid also ob-jected to the De Witt editions' misprints and use of notes "here and there thrust into the body of the book not infrequently making nonsense of the story."[7] Reid's fury at De Witt may be explained not only by the loss of money from the piracies, but also by the philosophical position taken by the "author" of the spurious works. For example, *Rangers and Regulators* (1870), presented as Reid's work by De Witt, displays an indulgent attitude toward slavery when the hero's faithful slave tears up his manumission papers, say-ing he has seen enough of abolition. Reid's strong position on slavery would have been sufficient reason for the dismay revealed in his epistolary attacks on De Witt.

One source of conflict in Reid's life has never been realized. His young wife, to whom he was entirely devoted, was miserable in the United States. The daughter of an English aristocrat, she did not share her husband's admiration for America. When she edited the Ollivant manuscript, she deleted the text of an abolitionist poem,

"The Nigger Shan't Rule Us," with the comment "too long and of
no interest to the reader in England." Ollivant crossed this remark
out and wrote in reply: "Rubbish and nonsense—Mrs. R always
hated America—even as her husband loved it—hence her objection
to everything illustrative of that noble country. C. O."

Despite his complaints about publishers and money, and his
wife's antipathy, Mayne Reid was delighted to be in America again.
Shortly after moving to New York City, he wrote to Charles Ollivant that "the people, the grandeur of everything keep me in constant wonder. It has fully borne out my belief in the republic. London and Paris both bound together would not equal New York in
metropolitan greatness. If America as a nation can hold together,
the old world must go under."

Reid continued to maintain a strong reputation in America. His
audience ranged from the masses who purchased the ephemeral
Beadle and Adams "dime novel" versions of his romances to those
with more substantial libraries. In 1868 an expensive illustrated
"Library of Travel and Adventure" published by James Miller contained a total of twenty-seven Reid titles selling for $40.50. But
Reid, not content to pursue a single path, decided to engage in
another literary adventure reminiscent of his *Little Times* experi-
ment, but on a grander and even more ambitious scale: *Onward: A
Magazine for the Young Manhood of America.*

The complete story of *Onward* would require a volume to itself,
and only the barest outline can be given here. To aid him in this
venture Reid enlisted Ollivant as his secretary and assistant. Charles
sailed eagerly from Liverpool on October 14, 1868, combining his
devotion to Reid with his enthusiasm at seeing the country he had
imagined from Reid's romances. The bustle of urban New York was
a far cry from the western plains, but Ollivant records no dissatisfac-
tion with what America offered. With his assistance, *Onward* first
appeared in December 1868. Although Mrs. Reid claims that "every
number was made up from original matter" (p. 177), much is not at
all original. While the production of *Onward* was an heroic task,
making enormous demands upon Reid (who wrote everything in its
first three issues), there is little mystery about its eventual failure.
Onward did not receive popular support because it was not directed
at a specific audience; it became a pastiche of Reid's own writing,
past and present, plus that of contributors whose articles either
originally reflected Reid's own biases or were edited by Reid so that
they eventually did.[8] The range of *Onward's* contents indicates the

problem of direction to an audience. While "The Young Manhood of America" might be eager for backwoods adventure tales like "The Yellow Chief" (1, January 1869), chronicles of famous battles like "Chancellorsville" (2, November 1869), articles on natural history such as "The Vultures of America" (1, June 1869), and even a treatise on "Croquet," they would be less responsive to such attacks on the English parliamentary system as "Sham Representation" (1, February 1869). And few red-blooded American youths would have had great interest in such sentimental fiction as "Thessaly Claremont" (2, December 1869) or the lengthy narrative poetry of "The Purple Swallow" (3, January-February 1870).

As the editor of *Onward*, Reid was jealous and overly zealous, feeling that he must control and manipulate every facet of the magazine. He dissipated tremendous amounts of energy in editing the contributions to his magazine, but never acknowledged the identity of his contributors in the magazine's index, merely suggesting that the authors could be acknowledged later if their material had been well received. The enormous drain placed upon Reid at this time is evident from his correspondence; the handwriting is particularly crabbed, indicating perhaps both the haste and fatigue of the weakening author-editor.

The whole *Onward* period was a grim one for Reid. The first issue contained two full-page advertisements, but subsequent issues have none, despite Reid's personal efforts to attract advertisers. Reid was finally reduced to raising money however he could. Edward Denny, his young American assistant, became his partner by paying him $500 (which itself was raised on loan by using the copyright and stereotype plates of Reid's rulebook, *Croquet*). Despite all efforts, *Onward* expired with the issue of February 1870, and both Denny and Reid were unemployed. By this time Reid was a tired, shaken man—on the verge of collapse. During the time he was working on *Onward*, he refused to speak in public on the grounds that "I have the greatest aversion to appear before a public, however select, in the character of an elocutionist." This was not the man who had amused Edgar Allan Poe with his tall tales twenty years before or who electrified political rallies in England in the following decade. But after the collapse of *Onward*, Reid regained some of his former energy and confidence in his oratorical abilities. A pleasant *Onward* aftermath was an invitation extended to Reid to lecture on Lord Byron at Steinway Hall April 18, 1870—an invitation resulting from Reid's defense of Byron in *Onward* against Mrs. Stowe's attack (2,

286 - 87). Reid was proud that the invitation had been given by those he considered the elite of America, and he was determined to vindicate Byron, who had always been his hero both as a poet and a rebel. Reid's speech, while florid to modern tastes, was sincere and effective. He praised Byron's poetic genius and attacked his defamers, notably Thomas Moore. Laced with readings from Byron's poetry, the lecture (like most Reid endeavors) was a vehicle in which his personal views were in the foreground and his talents as actor-showman were displayed to advantage. Certainly the *New York Herald* review of the lecture cited by Mrs. Reid indicates that he received a warm reception—"the lecturer discoursed eloquently and was loudly applauded" (p. 189).

Back briefly in the public eye, Reid's return was short-lived, for he soon experienced a rapid physical decline. His Chapultepec wound began to fester; he was confined to St. Luke's hospital for some months, and nearly died. The blood poisoning and diarrhea were severe, but according to the Ollivant manuscript he recovered by sheer force of will (plus the "beef juice and brandy" he swore by). When he regained his physical health, he was left with an acute state of melancholia—a mental condition that was to recur throughout his life. Mrs. Reid writes that "his delusions daily increased—a consultation was held by the doctors, who gave it as their opinion that the only chance of Mayne Reid's restoration was to return to his native land. . . . They told Mrs. Reid that if her husband remained any longer in the United States he would end his days in a lunatic asylum" (p. 203).

Mayne Reid's last stay in the United States had not lived up to the promise of the first. He was penniless and only found passage money for the return voyage through a $600 subscription—once more promoted by the devoted Ollivant—of donations from prominent Americans. Now too he was faced with separation from Charles, whom he encouraged to stay in the United States to seek his fortune in the West. They were to be parted for two and a half years. The Reids sailed for England on October 22, 1870, but Mayne Reid's road to recovery would be long and difficult and he would never fully regain his energy and vigor for life or literature.

IV   *Retreat to England, 1870 - 1883*

The last phase of Mayne Reid's life begins with his return to England in the fall of 1870 and ends with his death on October 22,

1883. In these last years, Reid suffered from both mental and physical illness; he struggled to produce new material, publish his collected works, and syndicate his novels, and he finally entered semiretirement as an amateur farmer, writing nonfictional articles about the English countryside. For some time before his death he was crippled by his old war wound; at the same time he had mellowed somewhat from his adventurous and radical youth.

Upon his return to England in 1870, Reid's melancholia proved to be a serious and enduring psychological disorder. Hoping to revive the captain's spirits, his brother Sam and his brother-in-law the Reverend T. Cromie extended invitations to the Reids for an Irish visit. The Reids accepted and here Elizabeth met her husband's young niece, Helen Cromie, who soon became as enamored with the youthful Elizabeth as Charles Ollivant was with the captain. While Helen adored both her newly met relatives, her uncle was now in such a deep melancholia that he could not bear to be left alone; he was in constant dread of losing his reason, and probably had become addicted to the opiates administered to him during his last illness.

After returning to England, Reid spent some ten weeks in asylums in Derbyshire, but the strict rules of the first asylum, Dr. Smedley's Hydropathic Establishment, were "too confining" and he insisted on being moved to another institution. His improvement was slight at best, and so the Reids went to London for a consultation with Dr. Russell Reynolds, a brain specialist who prescribed a return to work.

The quality of Reid's work both before he left the United States and after he returned to England shows that his mental state seriously affected his writing. His correspondence from this period reveals his desperate efforts to create "new" material, and also discloses his physical and mental stress. On September 22, 1871, he wrote to the editor of *Cassell's* that "if you give me a chance I will try to do my best, and I think either the *Headless Horseman*, or the *Lone Ranche*, (my last two attempts at romance writing), will show that I have not yet lost the art—whatever of it has ever belonged to me." Obviously Reid forgot that *Headless Horseman* had already appeared serially in England more than three years before this letter was written (in *Penny Miscellany* beginning July 11, 1868).

During this period of chronic mental illness, Reid attempted to publish his stories in *London Society*, and the tone of his letters to the editor, Henry Blackburn, pathetically documents Reid's state of

health and finance: "Many thanks for your kindness in sending me
the cheque of £4 which quite satisfies me. I shall send you in some
other articles subject to your approval but if I only knew the exact
style of paper that would suit you I think I could find it in the *reper-
toire* of my brain which I find is still strong enough for sketch-work,
though not for a prolonged effort. It is my poor heart that is out of
joint more than my brain." The "article" Reid mentions in the
letter was the story "The Maniac Skater"—not new at all, but a
revision of "The Mad Skater," which had appeared in *Onward* (1
[June 1869], 447 - 81), as the work of "Homer Greene of
Poughkeepsie, N.Y." Reid continued republishing *Onward* material
under his own name. *London Society* of November 1872 (22, 458 -
63) contains "Brother Against Brother," which is nearly a word-for-
word reprint of a story with the same title that appeared in *Onward*
February 1869 (1, 102 - 07). Many of the stories published at this
time by *London Society,* including two anonymous works, "Ghost,
or Grizzly?" and "Captured by Confeds," were later included in the
posthumous collection *The Pierced Heart* (London 1885).

In an attempt to revive his literary career, Reid wrote to Frederic
Chapman of Chapman and Hall on October 17, 1871, about a projected series of travel stories. The idea of a periodical publication
still obsessed Reid, and he suggested that "in *short* a periodical
which would from week to week instruct . . . in a sparkling and
lucid style *would assuredly be read.*" Reid proposed that Chapman
and Hall initiate such a publication with the captain at the helm:
"if you will establish such a periodical and make me the manager I
will neither be hard to please nor hard to pay. I know from experience you will treat me well." No such journal ever appeared,
but some of Reid's travel stories were published in *Field* in 1872. In
these articles, Reid appears to be trading on his reputation as an expert on Americana (although they are more likely based on research
than on any personal experience) and much of the writing is a mere
pastiche of his earlier works, dating as far back as the 1847
"Sketches by a Skirmisher." Clearly Reid's inspiration has left him,
and the pattern of repetition and self-plagiarism characteristic of
these years dominates his writing for the rest of his career.

Reid wrote no new novels until *Death Shot,* which ran serially in
the *Penny Illustrated Paper* in 1872 and appeared as a book in 1873.
In 1874, a second edition of the novel was published; the preface to
the new edition states that "this romance, as originally published,
was written when the author was suffering severe affliction, both

physically and mentally. . . . Dissatisfied with the execution of the work, the author has remodelled—almost rewritten it." But a comparison of the two texts shows that the revisions did not improve the original; the same story is retold but with more prolixity and less clarity. The addition of melodramatic, florid, and exotic embroidery probably indicates that Reid had not yet recovered sufficiently from his melancholia to have a critical perspective on his own work.

About this time, Reid began plans for the publication of his collected works, and Mrs. Reid states that by June of 1874 he had finished repurchasing his copyrights (p. 213). Two editions of his collected works appeared in the next few years; Ward & Lock published fifteen volumes in 1875 and Routledge, eighteen volumes in 1878. With them Reid's lagging finances improved slightly. While his financial situation and his mental health were somewhat better, he was physically disabled by recurrent illnesses resulting from his Chapultepec wound. In October 1874 the wound flared up dangerously. His illness was compounded by blood poisoning, and he nearly died. Reid never completely recovered from this attack, which left him on crutches for the rest of his life.

Largely unable to produce new work, Reid husbanded his literary assets and discovered newspaper syndication as a means of augmenting his income. He tried to interest the editors of provincial papers in his work by touting *Gwen Wynn*, a new romance written for serial publication, as an "English novel, the scenes to be laid here on the Wye River . . . a *mystery* . . . although a story of home life, and present time, I shall make scenes and incidents as exciting as any I have dealt with in forest or in prairie."[9] Those editors who accepted *Gwen Wynn* subsequently were approached with requests to serialize older works (many of which were revised and expanded versions of material that had appeared in *Onward* some ten years earlier). In this correspondence, Reid made syndication attractive to the provincial papers as well. While claiming that he received from £20 to £30 per paper per week for *Gwen Wynn*, he stressed that this simultaneous publication of a work in different parts of the country enabled a small paper to pay much less for a shared work than it would have to pay for an exclusive interest.

The correspondence about syndication continued for several years, but Reid was not totally committed to it as a means of support. Always in financial straits, he once more reached out across the Atlantic to capitalize on his American "connections." In January 1879 Reid began corresponding with New York newspapers, hoping to become an "English correspondent" able to inform American readers of the details of English politics. Unfortunately, his offers were not accepted and he continued to live a life severely limited by economic restrictions.

He tried to recover some of life's pleasures by taking a country house at Ross in Herefordshire. Again he named his home "The Ranche," perhaps in fond memory of the early years in Mexico and the pleasant life at Gerrard's Cross. Here he raised parti-colored sheep and Mexican potatoes, generally playing the part of rancher and countryman that seemed to remind him of the past, and from which he drew some consolation. However, crop failures were soon added to ill health, and in a final blow to his pride he was eventually reduced to secretly taking in a genteel lady boarder to help make ends meet. Despite this, he managed to keep up appearances when he visited London where he became something of a figurehead at the Langham Hotel and evidently still made a striking impression on those who met him. A ·New York lawyer, Jared Harrison, remembered meeting Reid at the Langham in 1880. Twenty-five years later Harrison's remembrance of the sixty-two-year-old Reid was strong enough to inspire a letter to the *New York Times* in which he described Reid as "a most charming gentleman. . . . He was a slight man of pleasing, intellectual appearance, walking with much difficulty, aided by a crutch, the result of a disability occasioned by a wound received in the Mexican War" (December 1, 1905, p. 837). Harrison and other of Reid's friends (moved by his plight and cognizant of his Mexican War service) later helped Reid get $2,400 in back pay and a pension from the United States government that finally was granted in September 1882. Reid certainly needed the money. His ill health and financial reverses provide the constant theme of his letters from 1880 onward.

While Reid wrote little new fiction after 1870, his nonfiction efforts included twenty-six informative articles on "The Rural Life of England," which appeared in the New York *Tribune* from April through September 1882. These articles are written with great enthusiasm, and the sustained quality of the first twenty-four, written long after his creative ability had vanished, shows that he still was able to write factual descriptions with some skill. Because of his lasting affection for America, Reid was particularly interested in the effect of his "Rural Life" series on its American audience. On July 16, 1882, Reid wrote to his American publisher Beadle and Adams: "how my correspondence is being received by the

American people I know not. Perhaps when you are writing to me, you would kindly say whether it produces a favorable effect or not."[10] Despite Reid's interest in extending the series, the subject was not inexhaustible, and the quality of the last two articles, "The Best Sort of Englishman for America" and "Naturalists' Field Clubs and Archaeological Societies," shows a marked decline in both content and style. Over Reid's protests, the *Tribune* cancelled the series with the issue of September 24, 1882.

In 1883, the Reids moved to London, where his health continued to decline. Up to the last he retained his love for America—that "far fair land," as he described it in one of his last letters. There Thomas Mayne Reid had become Captain Mayne Reid; the influence of America—its beautiful landscape, its potential for stirring adventure, and most of all its egalitarian political and social philosophy—had been a powerful shaping factor on his life and works. When he died on October 22, 1883, he had contributed little of belletristic substance, but he had forged an image of America and other lands of adventure that was to influence several generations of readers, both old and young.

CHAPTER 2

Reid and Romance

I Author and Genre

MAYNE Reid turned often to America, the land of his early adventures, for his fictional setting. While Reid eventually wrote about other exotic lands as well as the English countryside itself, his fantastic adventures in America and his detailed descriptions of that land distinguish his fiction from that of all other contemporary popular authors. In choosing America as the primary setting for his tales, Reid satisfied the demands of his ego while capitalizing upon the tastes of English and American readers. Drawing upon his own adventures as a young man, he was able constantly to relive and embellish those adventures—turning them into fantasies that rapidly distorted the actual experience. Reid simultaneously appealed both to English readers' interest in distant lands and to American readers' need to read romances that glorified themselves and their country; by so doing he was able to support himself with his pen for the rest of his life.

Reid's work is difficult to assign to any one category: novel, romance, adventure tale. His manner also escapes easy definition. To some extent he is a local colorist, resembling the writers of this school in looking carefully at particular geographic areas and attending to such things as the racial complexity of their population. Dealing with a locale familiar to him that he wishes to immortalize, Reid follows an essentially romantic impulse that assumes the author-creator has the power to confer "immortality" on a region, yet his techniques remain realistic. By insisting on verisimilitude both in setting and in the delineation of minor characters, Reid also resembles the local-colorists who believed that environmental factors influence human actions. However, Reid's local-color characteristics are diluted by sensationalism and sentimentality in plot structure and portrayal of major characters, while even his lov-

42

ing descriptions of the Mississippi and Wye rivers often appear to be apotheosis either for its own sake or for purposes irrelevant to the actions and characterizations of the story. This tendency to subordinate plot and characterization to naturalistic detail imparts a digressive quality to much of his fiction.

The comparison of Reid to Cooper is often made, although he also resembles Defoe, especially in what Ian Watt describes as the "total subordination of the plot to the pattern of the autobiographical memoir [which is] as defiant an assertion of the individual experience in the novel as Descartes' *cogito ergo sum* was in philosophy."[1] Yet Reid's heroes do not fit neatly into Defoe's pattern, for while the world of Robinson Crusoe is largely asexual, sexuality and the pursuit of woman pervades Reid's work. His heroes resemble Richardson's Lovelace, whose sole conception of sex, according to Watt, is governed by "the metaphor of the hunt" (p. 231). Reid's intense individualism was no doubt strengthened by his experiences in America, the land which glorified the individual, and certain of his fictional adventures could have taken place nowhere except in nineteenth-century America. Significantly, his only "historical" novels are set in revolutionary England where he tries to upset the traditional English preference for Cavalier chivalry. Reid, as might be expected from his radical politics, was a complete Roundhead.

Yet despite his concern for verisimilitude and attention to detail, Reid is really a romantic who may best be understood according to Northrop Frye's definition of romance as mythos rather than as tradition. Frye believes that "the romance is nearest of all literary forms to the wish-fulfillment dream, and for that reason it has socially a curiously paradoxical role. In every age the ruling social or intellectual class tends to project its ideals in some form of romance, where the virtuous heroes and beautiful heroines represent the ideals and the villains the threats to their ascendancy. . . . Yet there is a genuinely 'proletarian' element in romance too." Such a description might have been tailored for Reid, whose romances are indeed curiously paradoxical—full of fantasy and yet promoting extremely proletarian views despite the aristocratic nature of their heroes. Frye further claims that "the perennially childlike quality of romance is marked by its extraordinarily persistent nostalgia, its search for some kind of imaginative golden age in time or space."[2] That his contemporaries were aware of this quality in Reid's work, especially his creation of a "golden age in time and space," is apparent from the remarks of an anonymous critic in the London *Times:* "The very titles of the books are enough to stir the blood. 'The Scalp Hunter,' 'The Headless Horseman,' 'The White Chief'—what a vista they open up of wild adventure, of mystery, of savage heroism! There is in these books such a delightful disregard of the limitations of time and space, such a scorn of mere mundane probability, such an unerring instinct for the magnificently absurd, that they would satisfy even 'Ouida's' canons of romance" (October 24, 1883, p. 9).

By almost any critical canon Mayne Reid would have to be classified as a writer of romance rather than as a novelist. Readers of his works would agree that they fit Frye's criterion that "the essential element of plot in romance is adventure, which means that romance is naturally a sequential and processional form. . . . The central form of romance is dialectical: everything is focussed on a conflict between the hero and his enemy" (pp. 186 - 87). The characteristics of Mayne Reid's adult fiction are those of the romance mythos developed by Frye; it is appropriate that Reid often chose an Edenic America as his "golden age in time and space."

II   *Exotic Mexico and the Wild West*

Mayne Reid began his adventures in America; when he came to transcribe them into literature the pattern into which they fell generally followed the chronology in which they had been experienced. Discounting some fugitive poetry and "tales" written under various pseudonyms, the foundation for his work begins with his encounter with Mexico. English-speaking but not American born, he responded even more excessively than an American might to the exotic scenes, strange customs, and colorful characters he found during his tour of duty with the American army. These early romances are characterized by fast-paced adventure to which characters are often subordinated and a picture of the land which often looms larger than either plot or character. These are the characteristics of Reid's first adventure-romance, *The Rifle Rangers* (1850), which in turn he used as a seemingly endless source of theme and variation in his subsequent works.

The West depicted by Reid also appears to have been derived from his experience, although it was partly colored by his mythopoeic vision of America. With the exception of *Rifle Rangers,* most of Reid's novels were written years after he had left the American West and so his depiction was veiled by time and distance and given a dreamlike quality which recalls D. H. Lawrence's admission that "it is perhaps easier to love America passionately when you look at it through the wrong end of the telescope across all the Atlantic water."[3] And so while violence, murder, and mayhem abound in the western romances, their depiction had a strong power to attract both English and American readers. It was an attraction deriving from a generally accepted myth that transcended reality—a myth comprised of exoticism, power, freedom, and manifest destiny. This mythos was exploited by Reid in all the works with an American setting; the actions and characters were endlessly repeated but the vision remained constant.

III "Sketches by a Skirmisher": The Basis for Romance

Mayne Reid's writing always follows a pattern that utilizes formula plots and characters recurring in only slightly altered form throughout the canon. The autobiographical base for this formula was established early in his career with "Sketches by a Skirmisher," which appeared in *Spirit of the Times* beginning May 1, 1847, under the pseudonym "Ecolier." These early "Sketches" are a pivotal work; they signal the final phase of Reid's brief journalistic career and the beginning of his emergence as a writer of romance. By following the development of "Sketches" we can see Reid developing his formula for fiction—its relationship to his actual experience and to his fantasies—that would serve him for the rest of his writing career.

"Sketches by a Skirmisher" were written while Reid was serving in Mexico as a second lieutenant in the First New York volunteers. They were direct dispatches from Mexico, and document Reid's firsthand experiences in the Mexican-American War as well as his observations of the country, its people, and customs. The contents of the first dispatches, "The Sand Hills of Vera Cruz," "The Rancho and the Ranchero," and "An Encounter with Girls not Guerillas," comprise a veritable rough draft of what eventually became the first chapters of *War Life* (independently printed in New York in 1849) and *Rifle Rangers* (1850).[4]

Reid opens with the careful description characteristic of his work for its wealth of detail about the terrain of Mexico and the discomforts encountered in writing amid battlefield conditions—all of which successfully evoke the "spirit of the place." "The Sand Hills of Vera Cruz" begins: "You live in the cold North. You have seen the snow piled into fantastic shapes by the strong winds. Fancy these snow hills an hundred feet high, of a dusky, yellow hue, and you may form some conception of the hills that surround Vera Cruz."[5] Reid also describes a Mexican house: "The sides of the rancho are formed with long cane. . . . The roof of the rancho is a thatch made of leaves. . . . When the cold 'norther' blows, the sides of the rancho—at other times as open as a birdcage—are protected by large mattrasses [sic]" (p. 110).

After thus setting the scene, Reid as war correspondent relates various adventures of the American forces. The first event takes place in "An Encounter with Guerillas" when the Americans are sent by their superior officer to scout for mules to be "conscripted" into the American army. "On the 10th I was sent into the interior to collect some mules. . . . As we could not find the owner, we were under the necessity of borrowing without leave, according to the usage of war" (p. 110). But not all of the "Sketches" are directly concerned with the events of the war. In "An Encounter with Girls, not Guerillas," Reid directs his attention to the family of Señor Juan S———, whose daughters, the half-sisters Catalina and Inez, are lighly sketched: Catalina, "proud, haughty, her dark eye flashing . . . there was a slight expression of disdain (I thought so) in the curling of her swanlike neck," and Inez, "of lighter temperament, full of smiles . . . fair-haired and sunny eyed." In the later fictionalized accounts of *War Life* and *Rifle Rangers*, Señor Juan S——— becomes Don Cosme Royales, the sisters become Guadelupé and Luz, and the mule-hunting assignment initiates the adventure-romance, as the girls become the sweethearts of Captain Henry Haller and his lieutenant, Edward Clayley. Señor S——— of "Sketches" is the proud Spaniard who proclaims, "no Mexicanos—Somos Espanoles—Castellanos"—a gesture which Don Cosme repeats in *War Life* and *Rifle Rangers*.

IV   *Expanding the Adventure: War Life*

The "Sketches" of May 1 fill four newspaper columns; the total dispatches comprise a scant twenty-three columns. *War Life*, the first fictionalization of these events, is seventy double columns long. The additional length comes from the creation of an adventurous plot and much descriptive detail. The plot of *War Life* is essentially

the same as that of the first volume of the later *Rifle Rangers:*
Henry Haller enlists in a volunteer regiment; contests a villainous
Frenchman, Dubrosc, to become elected its captain (a contest won
with the help of a backwoods character, Bob Lincoln); lands at Vera
Cruz; is sent on a scouting party for mules; rescues the lovely
daughters of the Spanish hidalgo; has various encounters with Mexican guerillas; and wins the love of Guadelupé Royales whom he
leaves behind at the call of duty—"onward to Mexico City!"

In terms of clarity of plot and character delineation, *War Life* is
in some respects a more polished work than *Rifle Rangers*. For example, it contains an explanatory first chapter informing the reader
that the villain Dubrosc is really a spy in the service of Santa Anna,
sent to infiltrate the American troops and make himself more useful
to the Mexican cause by getting himself elected as an officer in the
American forces. (The motivation for Dubrosc's villainy is not
revealed in *Rifle Rangers* until the closing chapters.) And *War
Life*'s second chapter, an inset "Horatio Alger" story, describes the
waif Little Jack who has been mistreated by his uncle and sent out
on the streets of New York to beg and hence to be befriended by
Haller. Although Jack becomes an important minor character in *Rifle Rangers*, he is never so fully depicted in the later work.

Reid's natural mode was that of raconteur rather than creator and
he could not sustain his distancing pose of the impersonal narrator.
For after these introductory chapters, *War Life*, in spite of being
written in the third person, becomes even more strongly
autobiographical than the version in "Sketches." We see this when
the scene shifts to New York in November 1846, where on a miserable wintry day Henry Haller, fingering his last coin, finds out
that his manuscript has been rejected by a publisher who advises
him to produce " 'something rich and racy; here a murder, there a
seduction; bring in the theatres, the gambling houses and the
———' " (p. 8). But Haller cannot degrade himself to write such
trash; his author explains why in a revealing autobiographical
passage, especially interesting considering that "A Poor Scholar"
was one of Reid's early pseudonyms: "Here a shade of despondency
passed over his features. Gently born, tenderly nurtured, and highly
educated, Haller was without a profession, if we except the barren
and precarious calling which is the resource of many a poor scholar"
(p. 9). The autobiographical parallel, though anachronistic, is apparent in a letter quoted by Elizabeth Reid dated January 29, 1848
in which Reid complains to his father about his lack of literary

success and protests that "amid the charlatanism and quackery of the age I found I must descend to the everyday nothings of the daily press" (p. 81).

War Life shows itself to be the skeleton of *Rifle Rangers*, just as its embryo is to be found in "Sketches," and hence the three works represent three steps in Mayne Reid's creative process: from straight first-person reporting, to third-person narrative closely identified with his life, to first-person narrative slightly more fictionalized. Thus we observe Reid developing his formula for fiction.

V   *The Finished Product: Rifle Rangers*

By 1849 Reid had left the land of his American adventures en route for European revolutions; the "Sketches" of 1847 that served as the basis for *War Life* were to become the full-blown English publication *Rifle Rangers*, whose first edition filled two octavo volumes. Again, the greater length results from increased complexity at the plot level and the addition of more detailed descriptions of the surroundings.

The author's preface to the first edition is a useful document for a study of the relationship of Reid's life to his work; it suggests that he uses the actual events in his life as a foundation for his fiction and that he deliberately encourages confusion between the "author" who "served in the American Army during the late war between Mexico and the United States," and who writes "partly from his own personal experience" and partly from that of a "comrade; who, in these sketches is represented in the first person." Now certainly Reid is both "author" and "comrade," and this bifurcation of characters suggests the way in which Reid altered his material for his first English audience as well as the manner in which his imagination functioned to create a fictionalized hero out of his own personal experience. His separation of himself from his fictional hero is a thin gesture of denial, for Henry Haller is—in his manner of speaking, his concern for nature, his romantic involvement with extremely young girls, his republican sentiments, and even the details of his dress—certainly Mayne Reid.

In his preface Reid also declares his own interest in topography through the naturalistic detail that will figure so heavily in this and all subsequent works, stating that "while campaigning in that country [Mexico], his [Reid's] mind was forcibly impressed with its wild picturesque scenery, as well as by a thousand interesting pecu-

liarities in the character, costumes and customs of its inhabitants."
He again establishes the relationship of his fiction to experience by
stating, "most of the scenes selected are those of a stirring nature,
occurring to the writer and his comrades while engaged in
successive skirmishes with the *guerilla* of Cenobio, and the *jarocho*
band of the robber-priest Jaruta." Finally, Reid insists that the incidents are not fictions—"allowance made for a poetic colouring
which fancy has doubtless imparted. The characters are taken from
living originals, though most of them figure under fictitious
names." He also admits to a goal which will govern all his subsequent work: that of providing the English reader new pictures of
life and manners. This surely accounts for his constant depiction of
exotic places and people.

Regardless of the exact relationship of fact to fiction in *Rifle
Rangers*, what the reader encounters is a set formula—both of
characterization and structure—which will recur throughout Reid's
fiction, often without much variation. Roy F. Meyer has identified
the typical elements in Reid's fiction, which are fully illustrated by
Rifle Rangers: "The hero, visiting Mexico, falls in love with a Mexican girl whose father or brother is favorably disposed toward him
but somehow dependent on the villain, often a man of authority,
who of course has designs on the girl. The heroine somehow gets
lost, strayed, or stolen, and the hero goes in pursuit. The greater
part of the novel is then given over to the chase, which is enlivened
with numerous harrowing ordeals, hairbreadth escapes, and last-
second rescues. . . . Suspense is maintained until almost the last
page of the novel, when the hero emerges victorious over staggering
odds, the heroine is saved, the villain . . . is ignominiously
defeated, and the author hurries the tale to a close with a general
pairing off of all marriageable males and females."[7] However, in his
emphasis upon the importance of his setting, Reid always provides
more than plot action alone. To Meyer's description must be added
the intense focus on the landscape which Reid so often and so
lovingly described, and which makes his books a curious hybrid of
romance-adventure and travel guide. As the *Spectator* noted in
assessing the Reid canon: "Mayne Reid did possess one literary
faculty of a very rare and noticeable kind. He could create at-
mosphere as very few but the greatest storytellers have ever done.
The characters might be poor, and the story a jumble of horrors,
and the plot utterly unintelligible, but all the time the reader was
. . . conscious of residence under a new sky, of life amidst a strange

architecture, of the presence of dark-skinned natives who were not abstract 'natives.' . . . Captain Mayne Reid, for all his want of literary power, could when he wrote, transport himself to the country he loved, actually saw it and its people with his mind. . . . The result is a perfect illusion . . . and though we wonder why the people act in such a senseless fashion, we never weary, as strangers, of looking on at the novel and striking scene. This was Captain Mayne Reid's sole power . . . but he possessed it . . . in a unique degree, in such a degree that we gravely doubt whether any book whatever gives so vivid and accurate a representation of the land" (October 27, 1883, p. 1374).

Finally, any description of Reid's writing must take into account his republican spirit, which, fused with his escapist fiction and his particular love for the land, creates the unique quality of his work. In *Rifle Rangers*, this republican zeal is peripheral, for the emphasis lies on the adventures engaging the hero rather than on the politics that inspired those adventures. Nevertheless, in the United States the Mexican War was promoted as one to liberate a population enslaved by despotism—a cause which Reid-Haller would and did enthusiastically embrace.

Reid's recurrent elements of mode, plot, and characterization make their initial appearance in *Rifle Rangers*, which therefore provides the basis for understanding the rest of his fiction. The action of *Rifle Rangers* revolves around the adventures of its hero, Henry Haller, who as noted above is the thinly disguised Reid. As a prototypical Reid hero, Haller is at the center of the book and his adventures are the fictional recapitulation of Reid's actual Mexican experiences. The details of Reid's life fuse in his various fictional heroes to such an extent that they eventually will be confused with those of Reid himself. *Rifle Rangers* indicates that such biographical convolution was an inherent element from the very beginning of Reid's career. Haller, like Reid, is an officer in a volunteer company whose adventures begin in New Orleans where Reid himself first arrived when he came to America at twenty-two and to which he would return for the fictional setting of several of his American novels. Haller engages in a fantastic series of adventures, beginning with the Dubrosc duel and including such death-defying escapades as a fight with an alligator to save his future sweetheart.

In the creation of this fictional hero, Reid freed himself from the restrictions of time and space, while at the same time becoming a captive to his own imagination by reliving and retelling its one fantasy in different versions for the rest of his life. But Henry Haller's similarity to Reid goes beyond the events of the plot. Haller, like Reid, is obsessed with surfaces—of plant life and clothing and behavior—but seldom goes beyond appearance to examine interior psychological realities. Like Reid, Haller is content to concentrate on the details of dress rather than the fabric of being. Haller is attracted to the young naïve girl (a fictional event that anticipates Reid's marriage at the age of thirty-five to the fifteen-year-old Elizabeth Hyde). Haller is the arrogant and egotistical republican; again he is Reid.

Surrounding Haller is a gallery of characters, some of whom make their initial appearance here as prototypes for characters in later Reid novels: the mountain man, Bob Lincoln; the sidekick, Lt. Edward Clayley; the father of the romantic interest, Don Cosme; the dual heroines (one dark and the other light), Lupé and Luz; the mysterious woman disguised as a man, the wronged cousin Maria de Merced; the villain Dubrosc. Of particular interest because of their repetition in the canon are the mountain men, notably Bill Garey (*Scalp Hunters*) and Walt Wilder (*Lone Ranche*); the sidekick, Charles St. Vrain (*Scalp Hunters*); the dual heroines, Marian and Lillian Holt (*Wild Huntress*); and the girl disguised as a man, Isolina de Vargas (*War Trail*). Other characters such as the evil Catholic priest, the Canadian half-breed, and the stock Irishman, also will recur. Even the hero's trusty steed Moro appears by name in many of the later works.

From the opening in New Orleans the scene shifts to the Isle of Lobos where Haller and his company arrive en route to Vera Cruz. Lobos is the scene of Haller's first improbable adventure and near escape from death. Out for a walk after an evening wassail, Haller sees a mysterious skeleton and is assaulted by a stranger; his life is spared by a young woman's pleas (only her voice is heard). Some time later Haller awakens in the company of his men to learn that Dubrosc and a "boy" who was always in his company have deserted.

The scene next shifts to the Island of Sacrificios and then to Vera Cruz, around which most of the action will occur. Here Reid engages in extensive scene painting and renders the Mexican city in considerable detail: "The city stands on the very beach. The sea at full tide washes the battlements and many of the houses overlook the water. On almost every side a plain of sand extends to a mile's distance from the walls, where it terminates in those lofty, white sand-ridges that form a feature of the shores of the Mexican gulf. During high tides and northers, the sea washes over the surrounding sandplain and Vera Cruz appears almost isolated amid the waves" (I, 53). As the company disembarks at Vera Cruz, a mysterious shot is heard and the dread name of Dubrosc is once again invoked.

In the next chapter, Reid introduces one of his finest "humours" characters, Major Blossom, the gourmand quartermaster who would rather eat than fight and who seriously resents being sent on a dangerous expedition to find mules. Blossom is a kind of Falstaff to Haller's Hotspur and provides moments of great comic relief in a work where the elements of the actual adventure-romance are often strained. Blossom shows Reid at his comic best. Reid also relies on dialect and the "confusion of tongues" for additional humor, particularly in the mountain-man twang of Bob Lincoln (who confuses the Spanish *no entiendes* with "no in ten days") and in the two inset stories told during the rangers' drinking bout: "Lt. Sibley's Story of a Georgia Hotel," which adds dry wit to the description of infamous American hotels prevalent among contemporary British travellers; and the story of the "Guyas-Cutis" which features frontier humor based on rivalry between the states and focuses on two characters (who resemble Twain's Duke and Dauphin) gulling the public by exhibiting a supposed monster.

The next several chapters detail Haller's special mission: the search for mules. On their scouting party Haller and his men stumble across a gilded cage drawn and embellished from the original depicted in "Sketches," set down like a pleasure dome in the midst of the Mexican countryside outside Vera Cruz.

On the crest of the little hillock stood a house of rare construction—unique and unlike anything I had ever seen.

The sides were formed of bamboos, closely picketed, and laced together by strips of the palmilla. The roof—a thatch of palm-leaves—projected far over the eaves, rising to a cone, and terminating in a small wooden cupola, with a cross. There were no windows. The walls themselves were translucent. . . . The whole structure presented the *coup d'oeil* of a huge bird-cage, with its wires of gold! (I, 127 - 28)

The residents are Don Cosme Royales, his wife, and their two daughters. Haller first encounters the girls frolicking in their pool; he saves them from the attack of a cayman (alligator), thus endearing himself forever to Don Cosme and his wife. The rescue scene itself has been transformed; the earlier American version in *War Life* described the sisters bathing in the secluded pool before the alligator's attack as nude to the waist—and much was made of their voluptuousness, contributing to a strong sense of voyeurism. In *Rifle Rangers* they are clothed in sleeveless tunics and the hero's response is much more delicate. As the simple "d—ns" of *War Life* have become strengthened to epithet curses in *Rifle Rangers*, it is difficult to find a rationale for the tone and style shift. Perhaps the changes were made for English readers who would assume Americans to be a hard-cursing lot but who would not accept the nudity and more overt sexuality of the American version.

Haller develops an immediate romantic interest in the dark, lightly mustachioed Lupé, while Clayley becomes similarly enamored with her sister, the fair Luz. Lupé and Luz, like Haller, are prototypes for characters which figure throughout Reid's romances. Reid idealized young girls in art as well as in life and the description of the sisters in *Rifle Rangers* sets the tone for many similar descriptions that will flow from Reid's pen:

Their features, too, were alike . . . yet their complexions were strikingly dissimilar. The blood mantling darker in the veins of one, lent an olive tinge to the soft and wax-like surface of her skin; while the red upon her cheeks and lips presented an admixture of purple. Her hair too, was black; and a dark shading along the upper lip, soft and silken as the tracery of a crayon, contrasted with the dazzling whiteness of her teeth. . . . The other was the type of a distinct class of beauty—the golden-haired blonde. Her eyes were large, globular, and blue as turquoise. Her hair of a chastened yellow, long and luxuriant; while her skin, less soft and waxen than that of her sister, presented an effusion of roseate blushes, that extended along the snowy whiteness of her arms. These, in the sun, appeared as bloodless and transparent as the tiny gold fish that quivered in her uplifted hand! (I, 133 - 35)

Lupé and Luz are the predecessors of the many idealized young women who will appear in later Reid romances. Like Reid's other characters, they are, again, a peculiar and particular set of surfaces. Their motivations are either too transparent to be creditable, or totally inexplicable. They often function as decorative diversions for the autobiographical hero.

Haller and his companions are next fed a sumptuous meal that appears as if by magic, to the extreme delight of Major Blossom, and then led to Don Cosme's subterranean drawing room, described

as having a "gilded brilliance of some enchanted palace." Soon a
"norther" arises, mats are lowered to protect the gilded cage, and
Reid presents a disquisition on the violent and tempestuous exotic
storms of Mexico ranging from blasts of cold wind that send
terrified birds screaming from the creaking branches of trees, to sul-
phurous clouds, to sheets of lightning "and along with it the
crashing thunder—the artillery of heaven—deafening all earthly
sounds!" (I, 192).

The second volume of *Rifle Rangers* opens with Haller reflecting
on love. He decides that his love for Lupé is stronger than Clayley's
love for Luz (although Reid refuses to justify that sentiment by any
real psychological exploration). Love for Haller is mysterious and
somewhat enigmatic; he senses it in surface textures, but is unable
to explore its center. From this point of view, it is easy for him to
jump to jealous conclusions, and he does so. In his room that night,
Haller sees what he believes to be a portrait of Lupé and Dubrosc.
He imagines that Dubrosc is Lupé's lover, and, after considerable
agonizing, falls asleep, fatigued and despairing. The next morning
Haller coolly prepares to leave, still sunk in a senseless despair.
When Lupé reveals that the portrait is of her cousin (Maria de
Merced)—not herself—the two vow eternal love; Haller jumps into
his saddle and departs to rescue Lupé's brother Narcisso from im-
prisonment in Vera Cruz.

The next few chapters have Haller and the halfbreed French
trapper Raoul stealing recklessly into the fortified city in search of
Narcisso. They are discovered, imprisoned, and doomed to be gar-
roted when the bombardment of the city results in a hole being
blown in the roof of their prison, providing the convenient means of
escape. They rescue the boy Narcisso and return him to Don Cosme
before engaging in a series of adventures to resume the "chase"
motif as Haller and Raoul are captured by guerillas. The blindfolded Haller receives a mysterious letter from a mysterious lady
(Maria) informing him of a plan for his escape. Eventually Haller is
taken to the headquarters of the guerillas and Reid digresses into
descriptions of the locale, the food, local social customs, and a fandango.

Soon the Royales family also arrives at the guerilla camp and
Haller grows jealous and angry as he imagines complicity on the
part of the innocent Don Cosme. In the next sequence, Haller and
Raoul are freed through a complicated set of maneuvers involving a
confusion over the roles of Narcisso, Lupé, and Maria de

Merced—Haller alternately believing that each of them is responsible for his rescue.

As Haller, once again aided by Bob Lincoln, makes his escape, he sees Dubrosc accompanied by a young man with darkly beautiful features. Suddenly he realizes that this is Maria de Merced, the girl in the picture—Lupé's cousin. Her role in his rescue becomes clear at last, for we learn that she had been seduced by Dubrosc years before and forced to live as his wife although a legal ceremony was never performed. She is a wronged woman. With the appearance of Maria de Merced, Reid's cast of stock characters is nearly complete. Maria, as the girl in the guise of a youth, is most instrumental in saving Haller's life and she is, of course, in love with him. In her many manifestations, Maria represents a particular form of feminine strength and virtue in Reid's novels—a strength and virtue that are of slight threat to the autobiographical hero because they are possessed by a young girl who in the end drops her disguise and is once again a soft and vulnerable female. Although they are physical doubles, Maria and Lupé have very different personalities. In later works, these characters frequently fuse, either to serve like Maria as the heroine's foil (e.g., Eugénie Besançon of *The Quadroon*) or to become the hero's beloved, like Isolina de Vargas of *War Trail*.

The discovery of Maria's identity and predicament tempts Haller to remain and rescue her. But the chase pattern prevails and he flees with Raoul and Lincoln, the guerillas' bloodhounds in hot pursuit. Eventually the hounds force them up a cliff where Haller and company engage in man-to-dog combat, throwing the hounds over the precipice one by one. Although the dogs are out of the way, the men still must contend with their human enemies. This is accomplished by the use of an "Indian Ruse," in which their hats serve as decoys to confuse the guerillas while Haller and his men escape. An extensive digression permits the introduction of a terrifying electrical storm whose lightning bolts knock Haller out; he recovers in time to encounter a band of Jarochas (smugglers) led by the renegade priest Jaruta. Initially friendly toward Raoul, the Jarochas are influenced by the evil priest to become another species of enemy and once more Haller and Raoul are prisoners, while the crafty Bob Lincoln manages to escape. Jaruta—one of Reid's archetypal villains—takes great delight in contemplating the various means he might use to torture his victims, finally deciding to hang Haller by his heels from a tree which borders a deep crevasse. While Haller hangs over the cliff (calmly describing the fauna and flora below him), a shot is heard and suddenly the situation is reversed as Haller's lost company, guided by Bob Lincoln and Little Jack, defeats and hangs all the Jarochas. Haller beholds most of this action from his precarious vertical position over the crevasse.

Having defeated the Jarochas, Haller and his men now agonize as they behold other United States forces fighting the Mexican army. The battle is plainly in sight but proves inaccessible because of the mountainous terrain. As the losing Mexican forces begin to retreat over the side of a nearby cliff, Haller observes their stealthy escape and (despite orders to the contrary from his superior officer) dispatches his men to capture nearly all the runaway Mexicans, with the notable exception of their leader, El Cojo (Santa Anna). Haller becomes the unqualified hero of the battle and the man of the hour; Reid thus succeeded in creating a fictional hero who achieved the kind of uncontested military glory that he longed to claim as his own.

In Jalapa, as the victorious American forces celebrate the Mexican defeat and plan the final siege of Vera Cruz, Haller and Clayley are once again occupied with thoughts of Lupé and Luz. Haller becomes embroiled in an argument with the haughty and aristocratic Captain Ransom over a trivial matter; a duel of honor between them is cut short by another attack of guerillas and Haller kills Dubrosc. Haller and Clayley are invited back to the Royales home where the paired lovers are reunited. The closing scene shows Haller back in New Orleans reading a letter from Clayley who urges him to return to Mexico. Reid's parting comment reveals a rapid tonal shift as he asks his audience: "Reader, do *you* want me to come back?" The question was rhetorical; Reid was to return—essentially the same—in volume after volume for the next thirty-three years.

The 1850 edition of *Rifle Rangers*, as rehearsed above, remained substantially intact through its many editions (although some later ones—especially those which were pirated in America—eliminated some of the digressive material and often the extensive footnotes). Reid did make one significant change in the text himself. The 1860 edition (as well as most subsequent editions) begins with an eighteen-page chapter, "The Land of Anahuac," which serves as a lyrical prologue to the romance itself. This prologue has nothing to do with the plot; it contains only detailed description of the land

and a call to vicarious adventure. Like so much of *Rifle Rangers*, this preliminary chapter eventually became part of the formula for Reid's adult and juvenile fiction. It should be noted that Reid's enthusiasm for such prologues was not limited to his works set in exotic lands, as witness the opening lines of *Gwen Wynn* (1877): "Hail to thee, Wye—famed river of Siluria." In fact, the first such prologue was written in praise of "The Wild West" for *Scalp Hunters* (1851).

In "The Land of Anahuac," Reid attempts to draw the reader into the exotic setting of the novel by engaging in extensive romantic hyperbole. He directs this rhetoric to as wide a range of readers as possible: "Go with us tourist! Fear not. You shall look upon scenes grand and gloomy, bright and beautiful. Poet! you shall find themes for poesy worth its loftiest strains. Painter! for you there are pictures fresh from the hand of God. Writer! there are stories still untold by the author-artist—legends of love and hate, of gratitude and revenge, of falsehood and devotion, of noble virtue and ignoble crime—legends redolent of romance, rich in reality." It is difficult to image a single work of fiction that could live up to Reid's claims, and certainly *Rifle Rangers* does not. What this prologue can accomplish is a kind of disarming of critical perspective and submergence into the genre of escapist fiction. The chapter concludes with a final apostrophe that ultimately focuses on author and reader:

I am alone. My brain is giddy. My pulse vibrates irregularly, and my heart beats with an audible distinctness. I am oppressed with a sense of my own nothingness—an atom, almost invisible, upon the breast of the mighty earth.

I gaze and listen. I see, but I hear not. Here is sight, but no sound. Around me reigns an awful stillness—the sublime silence of the Omnipotent, who alone is here.

Hark! the silence is broken! Was it the rumbling of thunder? No. It was the crash of the falling avalanche. I tremble at its voice. It is the voice of the Invisible—the whisper of a God!

I tremble and worship.

. . . .

Reader, could you thus stand upon the summit of Orizava and look down to the shores of the Mexican Gulf, you would have before you, as on a map, the scene of our "adventures."

Despite its bombastic quality, this prologue is a curiously appropriate introduction to the series of improbable adventures to follow. Moreover, it is part of the "formula" to which Reid would return again and again in the creation of his world of romance. For *Rifle Rangers* included all the germinal elements of the Reid formula—plot, character, setting, and philosophy—which created his appeal to readers of his day.

Rifle Rangers, like so much of Reid's fiction, was a popular success, but failed to attract any significant critical comment. An American reviewer in the *International Monthly Magazine* comments only peripherally on the book itself while attacking a review in "one of the London journals" that had praised Reid as a "thorough Yankee soldier." In a bit of Anglophobic pique, the American reviewer comments, "the thorough Yankee, like many others much quoted abroad is a clever Irish adventurer, who was in the United States altogether some four or five years, engaged chiefly as a writer for the journals in New York and Philadelphia" (November 1850, p. 13). The reviewer here has focused on Reid's principal method, if not his particular fault; he would continue to capitalize on his American experiences for the next three decades, and to establish himself as an authority on the Americas.

The reviewer for *Bentley's Miscellany* also comments on Reid's overly active imagination: "all we can say is, that the author has gone through more extraordinary adventures within the time comprised in his narrative, than it has often fallen to the lot of man to encounter." More favorably disposed than the American reviewer, he admires Reid's flare for description and character delineation, forecasting great popularity for the young author. The reviewer's forecast proved true, and Reid's literary career was launched.

The success of *Rifle Rangers* was followed by the even more successful *The Scalp Hunters; or, Romantic Adventures in Northern Mexico* (1851). Its publication further secured Reid's position as the author of American romances and expanded the pattern that would become the foundation of the entire canon. While Reid retains Henry Haller and his intrepid steed Moro from the first novel, *Scalp Hunters* is not a sequel to *Rifle Rangers* but rather its temporal predecessor; Haller's adventures in *Scalp Hunters* are a consequence of his joining a trading expedition en route from St. Louis through Santa Fe to Chihuahua, an event that predates Reid's Mexican adventures by several years. In this case Reid's biography and his fiction are reversed; his own experiences with either the Stewart or Audubon expeditions of 1843 (which began in St. Louis) precede his adventures in Mexico as an officer in the First New York

Volunteers in 1847. His emergence from journalist to novelist explains why he chose to write about his war experiences first, but that he returned to an earlier period in his own American odyssey to create his next fictional work demonstrates both the extent to which his early fiction relies upon actual experience and the importance of the American West as his primary fictional setting.

As in the earlier novel, all of the action revolves around Haller, whose exploits are again used by Reid in a series of "hunt-and-chase" sequences, while the expedition provides the travel-guide formula that was to become such a staple in Reid's later work. But *Scalp Hunters* has an intrinsic importance in the Reid canon because of its shift away from a mere series of harrowing events towards a fiction that is informed by a political and social consciousness. The reasons for this are twofold: Reid moves his scene from despotic Mexico northward where American political and social ideals were prevalent, and he creates several uniquely memorable characters who figure in the thematic as well as narrative elements of the plot.

Reid's preface to the first edition of *Scalp Hunters* goes further to establish the correlation between his life and his fiction, but—again—it is a curious hybrid of gesture and retraction. After stating his regret that "my book exhibits no higher purpose than to amuse," he admits that he has "enamel[ed] its pages with a thousand facts—the result of my own experience" and then retreats—"let it *all* pass for a fiction—a novel, if you will—but, in return for this concession on my part, permit me to ask you—do you not think it a 'novel kind' of novel?" Reid's contention that he has made certain "novel" concessions is amusing when his first two works are compared; what Reid found, rather than made, was his own medium. The success of *Rifle Rangers* encouraged him to embark on another improbable, more fantastic, and faintly absurd fictional adventure. While deliberately capitalizing on a taste for the sensational in popular literature, Reid attempts to justify the savage elements in *Scalp Hunters*, again stressing a certain correlation between the factual author and the fictional work, "I am a coarse, crude, and careless writer. . . . If I *must* write, therefore, I am compelled—in order to interest—to lay more stress upon matter than manner." This confession comes dangerously close to the truth, for indeed there is little in Reid's manner beyond the sensationalism of escapist fiction to hold the reader's interest.

The prologue, entitled "The Wild West," describes in detail the

sublime and fearsome beauty of nature rather than the wildness of
the adventures to follow. Here the "lyrical" prologue of *Rifle
Rangers* is integrated into the work itself and an important shift occurs. In *Scalp Hunters*, Reid places his narrator-hero firmly in the
geography which is to have such a profound effect on him; the
reader feels the interaction between man and nature rather than the
distanced   worshipping   that   characterized   the   afterthought
apotheosis of *Rifle Rangers*. *Scalp Hunter's* beginning is more func-
tional to its action; there are no formal apostrophes from the
narrator, who the reader feels really is experiencing this grandeur.

With the scene thus set, we next see a restless Haller, newly arrived in St. Louis with a letter of introduction to Charles St. Vrain (a
real-life Santa Fe trader), with whom he joins forces. Haller's goals
are not purely adventurous; he seeks his fortune by becoming a
trader—and indeed makes a killing as his initial $10,000 investment
triples. In the company of St. Vrain and other traders, many of
whom are given the names of actual persons active along the Santa
Fe trail, Haller joins a large caravan headed for Mexico. The perils
that befall them en route seem particularly harrowing for a band of
merchants: a buffalo stampede gives Haller an early chance to establish his reputation as a western superman when he manages to
escape by mounting one of the stampeding animals and riding it to
safety, and in the very next chapter his horse Moro pulls him from
certain death in the quicksand he had overlooked while in hot pursuit of an antelope.

Safely in Santa Fe, Haller attends a fandango where he flirts ap-
propriately with the local señoritas; encounters a mysterious
stranger, Seguin the scalp hunter; and is stabbed in a brawl. St.
Vrain must move the wagon train on while Haller recuperates.
Chafing at this confinement, Haller enlists Godé (a French
voyageur in the mold of Raoul from *Rifle Rangers*) to accompany
him in search of the St. Vrain party. They hire a guide and rather
rashly set off across the desert on a trail known fearsomely as the
"Jornada del Muerte" (journey of death). Eventually the guide
deserts, and Godé is separated from Haller in a sandstorm. Next, we
accompany the solitary and feverish Haller through numerous perils
until he awakens in a strange house: Seguin's. There Haller meets
and falls madly in love with Seguin's twelve-year-old daughter, Zöe.
Haller's instant devotion to Zöe encourages Seguin to divulge his
strange history. As a mining engineer from New Orleans, Seguin
came early to New Mexico where he married his cousin Adele,

became wealthy, and fathered two daughters. The elder daughter, her mother's namesake, has been kidnapped by the Navajos at the instigation of the evil Spanish governor of the territory, who became enraged when Seguin's wife repulsed his adulterous advances. The loss of his daughter has turned Seguin into an Indian hater who collects scalps as much for vengeance as for money; he sees in Haller an ally who may help him in his search for Adele.

Together with Godé and Dr. Friedrich Reichter (a German botanist travelling in the West to classify flora and used by Reid to provide a convenient excuse for the proliferation of natural history descriptions loosely woven into the plot), Haller and Seguin's band begin their search for the Navajo's hidden city. Reichter, the travelling naturalist, is another of Reid's distinctive character types, appearing later in *The Quadroon* as Dr. Edward Reigart. The similarity of these names suggests an historical original, although no firm evidence exists. A famous German physician and botanist, George Engelmann, came to St. Louis in 1833. Reid may have known him, or he may have read about him or another German naturalist, Dr. Frederick Adolph Wislizenus, in Josiah Gregg's *Commerce of the Prairies* (1844).

Soon three other able members are added to the party to ensure its success: the "good" Indian Chief El Sol; the stalwart young trapper Bill Garey; and his companion, Rube Rawlings—a fearless, earless Indian hater. When the search party finds Adele they discover an unexpected difficulty—her years with the Navajos have "indianized" her. She has become their "mystery queen" or high priestess. Not even recognizing her father, she has to be "rekidnapped" in order to be rescued. Meanwhile, a Navajo raiding party has pillaged Seguin's home and carried off Mme Seguin and Zöe, which leads to a lengthy attempt at exchanging hostages. The apparent impasse is resolved by the timely arrival of St. Vrain and a rescue party, and love triumphs as Zöe and Haller's joy is shared by that of St. Vrain and Adele.

As the sketch above indicates, most of the characters or character types that first appeared in *Rifle Rangers* reappear here. Reid adds to this gallery a few new types that will serve as models for his later fictional casts. And in *Scalp Hunters* we witness for the first time the dual processes of fusion and bifurcation by which Reid achieves his most typical character variations. His own splitting of hero and author, as discussed above, may have provided the basis for this fictional device.

Of the characters that are essentially the same, Henry Haller is most evident. He has both the same name and the same predominant position in the narrative action. Haller here is the young Reid: newly arrived from Ireland in America, painfully aware of his lack of practical training for a life of rugged adventure, vaguely (at times embarrassingly) naïve in his initiation to American society. Unlike the earlier hero, the Haller of *Scalp Hunters* seeks not only after adventure but examines the adventures in light of their political and social overtones. Thus Reid achieves an integration of character, action, and message in a single hero who begins to resemble his author in nearly all respects.

Also reappearing as recognizable types from the earlier work are the young sisters, the fair Zöe and the dark Adele. Zöe is a mere child of twelve when Haller meets her, thus the biographical parallel is particularly interesting. Reid met his future wife, Elizabeth Hyde, in 1851 after the publication of *Scalp Hunters:* he was thirty-three, she was thirteen. Reid gave her a copy of the book and told her, "you *are* Zöe." Mrs. Reid relates that Reid himself thought their relationship was foreshadowed. If Reid believed in the "self-fulfilling prophecy," it might help explain the curious fictional anticipations we encounter when comparing his work with his life. (See *Captain Mayne Reid*, p. 127.)

That Zöe is fair and helpless and yet the object of Haller's affections evidences one of the frequent variations in Reid's fiction, as he would alternate between dark, strong women and fair, weak women for his fictional lovers. Of greater interest than Zöe is her sister Adele; she combines characteristics of Lupé and Maria de Merced of *Rifle Rangers*. As the darker sister she satisfies the role of Lupé; as the captive proud "Indian princess" she embodies much of the spirit and mannerism of Maria. Although she never dons the costume of a man, she has masculine power in the Indian culture to which she has been removed and her restoration to her white family serves as a bridge between the two worlds. Adele, the kidnapped child, also provides the basis for Reid's observations and commentary on the Indianization of captives.

As the father of the girls, Seguin is superficially another Don Cosme. But the differences far outweigh the similarities. Don Cosme was a mere functionary in the plot of *Rifle Rangers*, while much of the action of *Scalp Hunters* focuses both thematically and narratively around Seguin. The indignant "aristocrat" turned Indian hater as a consequence of Indian savagery (including the kidnapping of Adele), Seguin serves as a focal point for Reid's views on the savageness of some Indians. In many respects Reid's most original creation, Seguin is on the one hand a villain and on the other hand a sympathetic outcast from society, which may have appealed to Reid—himself the voluntary exile from his native land.

In *Scalp Hunters*, the earlier *Rifle Rangers'* backwoods character of Bob Lincoln splits into two distinct types: Bill Garey and Rube Rawlings. These two characters also demonstrate the distinction between Cooper's earlier stereotypic backwoodsman and the essentially more believable types that appear in Reid. In her study of Cooper, Kay Seymour House comments that "Cooper's America is composed largely of communities which are entities because they share something: a race, a religion, a sex, an occupation."[8] This is not true of Reid's characters, each of whom is much more adaptable than any of Cooper's. None of Reid's gentleman heroes, for example, is as helpless as Duncan Heyward, nor are his backwoodsmen quite such rustics as Natty Bumppo. Reid's backwoodsmen also are more realistic than Natty, and for the modern reader much of the interest lies with these backwoods characters although they lack the philosophical complexity to be found in Cooper.

Reid doubles Cooper's Natty Bumppo character with two hunter-trapper figures: one young and thus capable of being involved in the romance plot; the other old, wise, and detached from such foolishness. Bill Garey is the young trapper of *Scalp Hunters*, clearly cast in an heroic mold: "He stands leaning on his long straight rifle, looking into the fire. He is six feet in his mocassins, [sic] and of a build that suggests the idea of strength and Saxon ancestry. His arms are like young oaks, and his hand, grasping the muzzle of his gun, is large, fleshless, and muscular. . . . The countenance is not unprepossessing. It might be styled handsome. Its whole expression is bold, but good-humoured and generous" (I, 262 - 63). Garey, a young and unphilosophical Natty of the mountains, has an abortive romance with the Indian princess, La Luna, something that never could have occurred in a Cooper novel. This may be an example of Reid's greater knowledge of his subject than Cooper, for historically many of these rude trappers formed liaisons with Indian women, princesses and otherwise. Reid's character may be a romanticized portrait drawn from life, for a William Guerrier, known as Bill Garey, was a trader and frontiersman working out of Bent's Fort along the Sante Fe trail; he spoke Cheyenne, had a Sioux wife, and lived among the Indians.[9]

A more interesting backwoods character is the old trapper Rube Rawlings, a survivor of many an Indian attack and a confirmed Indian hater who keeps an accurate count of his Indian victims by notching the barrel of his trusty rifle "Tar-guts." Rube is almost completely a realistic character because of his savagery—a well-known trait among certain frontiersmen of the period, especially among those who had suffered at the hands of the Indians. And Rube has suffered: he is both earless and scalpless. He is a tracker of uncanny skill who develops his ability to the end of gaining revenge and Reid exploits his bloodthirsty deeds to the fullest. Yet Francis Edward Hodgins, Jr., is correct in his remarks about Rube: "He is so far removed from the stereotype, and toward a realistic characterization that he is willing at one point to sacrifice the hero to save his own neck, although this is treated as if it were all a mistake and Rube quickly reverts to standard form. Yet he represents a definite freeing of the old hunter character from the prison of stereotype, from the conventions of primitivism."[10] Rube appears under his own name in *War Trail* and *Guerilla Chief,* and similar characters (although without his savagery) include Old Ike of *Hunter's Feast,* Zeb Stump of *Headless Horseman* (who also figures in a short story, "Trapped in a Tree"), and Walt Wilder of *Lone Ranche.*

While each of Reid's backwoods characters is interesting, realistic, and believable, they all clearly lack the symbolic complexity of Natty Bumppo. Reid does not use his backwoodsmen to develop any profound moral themes; he is content to describe them as realistically as he describes the American flora and fauna. Such characters serve several purposes. First of course they provide local color, not only in their exotic buckskins and moccasins, but also in their speech and behavior. Their language differentiates them from the aristocratic yet democratic heroes of the main plot, and they indulge in traditional Western argot—calling themselves "child," and "hoss," their hands "claws," their outfits "possibles"—all accurate representations of the speech of their originals.

El Sol and his sister La Luna—the first "noble savages" in Reid's writing—are important for an understanding of the full emergence of this character type in *Oçeola.* El Sol is a rich Maricopa chief (although since he was abducted by the Navajos as a child and rescued years later by Seguin it is not clear how he accumulated his "gold and pearls") whose wealth has contributed to his nobility. Unfortunately, although loyal and courageous, El Sol is not believable. Educated at Oxford, world traveller, botanic scholar, fluent in many languages, perfect in the details of government as well as archery, he resembles no Indian that ever existed on this earth. Reid implies through El Sol that his "westernization" has made this savage noble—an idea that also will predominate in *Oçeola*. La Luna is a foil character to her brother. Unlike him, she is uneducated and her behavior is consequently more realistically "Indian." Yet through her active participation in the search party and her love for the young trapper Bill Garey, traces of the Maria de Merced character appear.

Despite Seguin's virulent hatred of the Navajos, most of the Indians depicted in detail in *Scalp Hunters* are more noble than savage. Although the tribe is described as perpetrating much gratuitous violence, including mutilations and other attendant horrors, both Dacoma (a high-ranking Navajo chief) and the venerable Navajo medicine man are shown as persons acting out of principle; they are real. Dacoma is the object of El Sol's vengeance for a vague crime committed in the past. Yet in his first appearance in the book he is described as "a picture more like some Homeric hero than that of a savage of the 'wild west' " (p. 182). The necessities of the plot make him brave, brutal, and licentious: his characterization stresses the first term while denying the second two. Similarly, as drawn by Reid, the old medicine man's desire to retain Adele (who has been with him for so many years) is understandable. He has a fatherly as well as a proprietary interest in her, and their parting evokes considerable poignancy. Thus *Scalp Hunters* presents some basic truths of human nature as well as natural history, recalling Hodgins's comment that "the Western had to have truth before it could have art, history before it could have literature" (p. 142). With *Scalp Hunters'* setting, characterization, and theme, Reid moves in this direction.

Scalp Hunters was even more favorably received than *Rifle Rangers*. As the first of many Reid novels to be noted by the *Athenaeum*, it occasioned a five-column review which devoted extensive space to quotations from the book, apparently in an attempt to convey to the reader its unique character as perceived by the reviewer. Its "shocking" rather than "romantic" adventures are nevertheless described as "full of fierce life and feverish interest." Haller is seen as a hero encompassing qualities from Hotspur to Romeo, and while acknowledging Reid's debt to Cooper and the Wordsworth of "The Borderers," the reviewer stresses Reid's ability to fascinate his readers (pp. 766 - 67). The reviewer in *Chambers's Journal* made similar comments, concluding that *Scalp Hunters* was "a production as original in its faults as in its excellences" (August 23, 1851, p. 126). Most of the unique character and original qualities discerned by these early reviewers would be repeated in Reid's subsequent adult works.

During the years 1852 - 54, Reid was largely occupied in writing adventure tales for the juvenile market. In 1855 he adapted the formula of the hunt-and-chase tale developed for this youthful audience in *The Hunter's Feast: or, Conversations Around the Campfire*, which uses the device described in the subtitle to expand the range of adventures. *Hunter's Feast* obviously appeals to audience interest in both adventure and natural history by pairing each actual hunt with a tale retold from the past (often set in different lands and describing different kinds of animals). The book is thus a transitional work—one not directed explicitly to boys, yet placing its adult characters in the same framework that had proved so successful with a juvenile audience.

With *The White Chief: A Legend of Northern Mexico* (1855), Reid returned to his "adult romance" formula—but with a slight difference. *White Chief* is one of the few nonautobiographical works in the Reid canon. It also is noteworthy as a transitional work, dealing as it does with both Mexican and far-western subjects and capitalizing on the interest in Indians evident from the reception of *Scalp Hunters*. Set once more in the isolated West, *White Chief* conveys an essentially political theme beneath its surfaces. All the superficial details—Indian tribal warfare; anti-Mexican prejudices and anti-Catholicism (particularly heightened by Reid's vehemence against the Church for its alliance with constituted authority against the forces of freedom and democracy); and the Byronic hero, who bears little resemblance to the Reid-Haller of previous works—serve to carry an explicit message: manifest destiny. As is often the case in the early works, Reid's factual notes are most revealing. The first edition of *White Chief* states: "It is somewhat curious that the name 'Americano' is given to the people of the United States by all Spanish Americans. The inhabitants of Mexico call themselves Mexican, those of Peru, Peruvians . . . but the name Americano is used only in reference to the Anglo-American race. One might read 'manifest destiny' in this exclusive appelation of the title" (III, n., 270 - 71).

White Chief is the first romance in which Reid achieves a distancing effect through use of the inset story. The entire narrative takes place more than a hundred years in the past when a civilization existed where now only the ruins of a deserted Mexican village set in the midst of the wild grandeur of nature give any indication of the "legend of San Ildefonso"—a legend that will comprise the story to be told. This distancing in time permits Reid to indulge in some fantasy, much gratuitous savagery, and considerable prophecy—both overt and symbolic—about America's manifest destiny.

Carlos, the hero, despite his Spanish name, was an American "cibolero" (buffalo hunter) living with his mother and sister in the midst of those who hated them as intruders and heretics—the Mexicans. Despite the widespread belief that Carlos's mother is a witch, one of the dual villains is full of lecherous desire for his beautiful sister Rosita. Thus Reid combines religious prejudice with sexual passion to heighten the sensational aspects as much as possible. When the Mexican villain arranges for Rosita to be kidnapped by his henchmen (disguised as Indians), he initiates the typical Reid hunt-and-chase plot. This plot allows Reid to set up a strange convolution of racial animosities. As usual, the Americans are the favored race, but here they are set down as total outsiders to deal with two sets of antagonists: Indians and Mexicans. Oppressed by the evil Mexicans, the Indians are wise enough to realize "their deliverers from the yoke of Spanish tyranny would yet come from the East—from beyond the Great Plains" (I, 49). Carlos is the symbolic precursor of this forthcoming deliverance through a series of incidents including a battle in which he kills the slayer of the Waco Indian chief. The tribe then selects him as their "white chief" and he takes the role of their leader and savior from the arch-villainous Mexicans. So in this strange juxtaposition of racial hatreds, it is the "free American" allied with the native American against the "tawny Spaniards."

Aside from his symbolic alliance with the Indians, Carlos functions as a hero with a strange mixture of characteristics. Partly Byronic, Carlos is a romantic with an eye for picturesque scenery: "To him the open plain or the mountain cave was alike a home. He needed no roof. The starry canopy was as welcome as the gilded ceiling of a palace" (II, 145). Yet Carlos (like Defoe's heroes) hopes to accumulate a fortune by plying his trade as a buffalo hunter. These riches will serve a double purpose—not only to win the hand of Catalina, the aristocratic daughter of a standard Reid "rico"—

but also to give him the power to fulfill his manifest destiny role as forecast by Reid. The autobiographical and Byronic echoes recur in Carlos who, like Reid, was a stranger in a strange land. As he admits to Catalina: "For me there is no world. I have no home. Even among those with whom I have been brought up, I have been but a stranger—a heretic outcast" (II, 248).

As for Catalina, she is an intrepid, intelligent heroine. Possessing a refined taste exemplified in the beautiful landscaping of her home, she remains true to Carlos despite all the canards spread about him by the Mexican villains. When he is locked up in the Presidio dungeon, disconsolate at the death of his mother (whose torture at the hands of soldiers and priests he has been forced to watch), and ready for suicide, Catalina renews his resolve by outwitting his guards and throwing gold, a knife, and an encouraging note through his cell window. Catalina de Cruces is Reid's fantasy señorita to whom love gives a "strength and sublimity, . . . a true passion—unselfish, headlong, intense—usurping the place of every other, and filling the measure of the soul. Filial affection—domestic ties—moral and social duty—must yield. Love triumphs over all" (III, 188). Catalina enacts this fantasy in her relations with Carlos; going against her community and her father, she joins forces with Carlos (her kindred courageous and resolute spirit), provides horses stolen from her father for the escape, and proves herself worthy to become Carlos's mate.

As the rapid pace of the narrative accelerates, Carlos vows vengeance against the village on the corpse of his mother and suddenly disappears. Then, with Chapter Twenty of Volume III, Reid reappears to remind us that all of the story we have read has been a response to a question about the fate of San Ildefonso—the weed-covered, ruined village now totally isolated from civilization and with no trace of its former inhabitants. Its fate was determined by the "White Chief," who returned at the head of five hundred Waco braves to wreak bloody vengeance on the village—soldiers and citizenry all destroyed; the village put to the torch; the priests executed; and the two chief villains set upon blindfolded wild mustangs which were goaded to leap from the highest cliff and be dashed to death on the rocks below.

So Carlos has achieved his goal. With wealth from looting the village and treasure promised by the Indians, he and Catalina can achieve another Reid fantasy; they move to Louisiana to lead a peaceful and prosperous life. Reid has exploited a romantic's interest in Indians to develop both plot and theme; Carlos has always been an American and his assumption of leadership with the Wacos was only necessary to explain how he was able to conquer the town. Indeed, here the Indians are the deus ex machina for plot and theme; they are not characterized beyond these functions.

It should be noted that Reid's work was not taken seriously by contemporary reviewers—it was "light literature" and received "light criticism." Thus the *Athenaeum*, Reid's constant reviewer, was not aware of any particular message in *White Chief*. As usual the focus of the review was on the breathless adventures as well as the accurate descriptions of American scenery "drawn not only with the hand of a master, but with a brilliancy and reality that prove them done from the life" (January 5, 1856, p. 12). The reviewer was correct: the American scenery Reid chose for his setting was the wild and dangerous West, which he describes in detail not only in the body of the work but also in the fifty-three pages of "Explanatory Notes" at the end of the third volume of the first edition. Reid knew this territory; his accuracy is apparent when he states that the headwaters of the Red River are on the Staked Plain rather than in the Rocky Mountains as they were shown on nineteenth-century maps. Ruined towns like San Ildefonso have been discovered and Reid turned such reality to his own purposes. He had an ideal hero made to serve both his own fantasies and his sincere belief in the value of American civilization, and he placed a strong woman by his side. The destruction of San Ildefonso is made to represent the decline of Spanish power throughout the continent: this is Reid's main theme and the rudimentary and confusing plot serves only to promote it.

The War Trail: or, the Hunt of the Wild Horse (1857) is the first of Mayne Reid's "adult" romances bereft of extensive explanatory and descriptive notes. Perhaps the readers no longer needed such comprehensive guides to the territory. In setting, plot, and characters, *War Trail* follows *Rifle Rangers* and *Scalp Hunters* with the exception that the treatment of the heroine is significantly different: she is strong, masculine, and very much in control. The book is divided into two sets of chases; American superiority remains the governing theme, and as usual the Indians fare a bit better than the Mexicans.

A group of American rangers have been sent to guard a conquered Mexican settlement against the ravages of the Comanches who are on the "war trail" of the title. Reid's autobiographical hero,

Captain Edward Warfield, leads this group of diverse characters (probably modelled on the Texas Rangers of the period). Their mission is "to extend the area of freedom" and thus Reid builds upon the incipient idea of manifest destiny first developed two years earlier with *White Chief*. The hero's allegorical name indicates the action the plot will take: Warfield on the *War Trail*, with diversions as needed to accommodate the love interest in the person of Doña Isolina de Vargas.

The action begins as Warfield chases a strange horseman who turns out to be Isolina—an expert cowgirl who speaks fluent French and charms him with her brains and wit as well as her dark beauty. Their relationship begins as Warfield shoots her horse out from under her. Instead of rescuing the heroine from danger as was the case in *Rifle Rangers*, the hero now has placed himself in jeopardy—will he have to replace her steed with his adored Moro? This causes some concern, for like the modern cinema cowboy, Warfield loves his horse as much if not more than his woman and although she has "*already divided my interest with Moro*," he is not anxious to give the horse up to her, "proud, beautiful woman though she may be" (p. 21).

Warfield, like all Reid heroes, subscribes to the lightning-bolt theory of love at first sight and he is mightily stricken by Isolina. Whenever he is not on the trail his thoughts are only of Isolina—but she is mysteriously aloof. Although they meet socially because of his errand to buy horses from her father for the use of the rangers, she displays little initial interest in his suit. A strange incident at a masked ball illustrates both Warfield's state of mind and the quality of the heroine. At the ball, Warfield observes a beautiful woman wearing a yellow domino dancing and flirting with one of the company dragoons. He is certain she is Isolina, but when she unmasks she is revealed to be a Negress. When she is forced to leave the ball in humiliation, Warfield feels both curiosity about her and pity for her (as well as relief that she was not Isolina after all). In the next chapter, Warfield himself dances with an equally lovely lady wearing a blue domino whom he again is sure must be Isolina. At unmasking time she is revealed as the same Negress and she taunts him for his lack of perception and for his attitude toward her race. Both hero and reader by this time are totally confused: perhaps the Negress really was Isolina playing tricks on Warfield and on her society as an indictment against the frailty of human nature and against racial prejudice.

Such philosophical problems soon disappear, however, as Isolina sends Warfield a note commanding him to prove himself by capturing for her the famous wild white horse of the prairies to replace the horse he has killed. This request sets up the hero-in-nature sequence, with its chase; contest with the elements and concurrent philosophizing about life; detailed description of the grizzly bear and its habits; a hand-to-bear combat and the hero's resulting fainting spell followed by rescue at the hands of his old friends from *Scalp Hunters*, Bill Garey and Rube Rawlings. Before returning with the prized white horse for his mistress, Warfield's group encounters a band of guerillas led by Ijurra, Isolina's wicked cousin. The reader will immediately note an echo of familiarity: Ijurra is in love with Isolina, whom he threatens to turn over to Santa Anna unless she agrees to marry him. The incident and the relationship are from *Rifle Rangers;* Ijurra is merely a repetition of Dubrosc, while Isolina is a fusion of the Lupé and Maria de Merced characters.

The first chase having ended with Warfield victorious, the ranger group answers the call of duty to move on; Warfield and Isolina have a tender parting very reminiscent of the end of *War Life;* he must return to his company because "I entertained the idea that I was aiding the designs of 'manifest destiny'—that I was doing God's work in battling against the despotic form" (p. 226). In the rangers' absence, Reid sets up the rationale for the second chase sequence, with careful attention to violence and sadomasochism. Once the village is unprotected, the guerillas attack, branding the foreheads of the women with the mark "U.S." and cutting off their ears. When the rangers receive word of this atrocity, they return at once and of course Warfield is fearful that this same fate has befallen Isolina. However, she is not in the village; she has been lashed to her wild white horse, which has had firebrands inserted into its haunches and been driven off across the prairie. As he begins his extended tracking chase, Warfield gives further evidence of Reid's Byronic influence by commenting: "Despite my heart's bitterness . . . I could not help thinking of the Cossack legend. The famed classic picture came vividly before my mind. Wide was the distance between the Ukraine and the Rio Bravo. Had the monsters who re-enacted this scene on the banks of the Mexican river—had these ever heard of Mazeppa?" (p. 268).

Aided by Rube's expert tracking skill, Warfield eventually discovers Isolina as an Indian captive and through a series of disguises and clever maneuvers, including establishing a friendship with

Wakono (son of the chief of the capturing tribe), he is able to rescue Isolina. No fainthearted maid, Isolina provides plenty of assistance by attacking her captors and leaping upon the white steed, who then joins Moro in a gallop across the prairie for an ecstatic reunion between hero and heroine.

The appeal of *War Trail* to contemporary readers came no doubt in part from the titillation experienced by stay-at-home readers exposed to its frightful but thrilling perils, as well as from the precise pictorial descriptions of the land that occur occasionally. No extant reviews of the book have been found. Certainly it is not noteworthy except as it indicates a pattern Reid would follow all too often in the years to come; repetition of both plot and characterization to the point that in many cases the reader is not certain if what is being read is in any respects original. Reid began his writing career by borrowing from his life. Those parts of it that had adventure and romance provided these qualities in his earlier works. But when he began to borrow from those works themselves, the life had gone out of his fiction, to reappear only fitfully when some different topic aroused his curiosity sufficiently for him to explore it rather than merely to repeat old tales.

This continuing circular accretion is apparent in *The Wild Huntress* (1861), for here Reid draws only briefly upon his memories of Tennessee for the opening scenes and then plunges immediately into a work composed largely on his previous patterns. Again the hero is Edward Warfield—not fresh from his conquest of Mexicans and their señoritas in *War Trail*—but set forward in time to the period when Reid-Warfield has been mustered out of service in the Mexican War with sufficient capital to purchase a homestead on the banks of the Obion River. En route he meets the handsome young backwoodsman Frank Wingrove, who is in love with Marian Holt, the dark sister (she has one-quarter Indian blood) and daughter of the mysterious Hickman Holt, a Tennessee squatter whose land Warfield has come to buy. When Warfield meets Marian's fair sister Lillian, the romantic pairings are established, but *Wild Huntress* adds a newly sensational aspect: the anti-Mormonism theme displayed by many of the British novelists and travel writers of the period who wrote about America. Thus the device used to set the typical hunt-and-chase in motion is the evil machinations of the villain Josh Stebbins (a Mormon "Saint"), who blackmails Hickman Holt into making one daughter "marry" him while he arranges to spirit the other away, presumably into the white slavery of Mormon polygamy. "Polygamy?" writes Reid, "No! the word has too limited a signification. To characterize the condition of a Mormon wife, we must resort to the phraseology of the *bagnio*" (p. 162). Such standard anti-Mormon canards naturally make the chase that ensues particularly feverish, for the double heroes' goal is to save their beloveds from a fate worse than death (or so it is drawn in terms of religious prejudice).

Although she shares the role with her sister, Marian Holt is a heroine even stronger than her predecessor Isolina de Vargas. She is an independent Diana who outwits the villain and goes to live off the western lands as a "wild huntress," inspiring the love of the noble Ute warrior Wakara, yet she remains committed to her love for Frank and to the rescue of her weak, fair sister Lillian from the Mormon fiends. In her strength, autonomy, and life in nature, Marian is at once Reid's fantasy heroine and his own androgynous projection. Much of the book's power derives from this combination; through it Reid briefly convinces us, as he was once convinced, that life in the wilderness can be free, strong, and restorative. Hence the formula ending, with Marian returning happily to the domestic hearth and joys of motherhood, seems an especially forced capitulation to social and literary convention.

Beyond this, much of what we find in *Wild Huntress* is all too familiar: the heroes travel westward on the trail of the missing sisters; the evil Arapahoes (led by their grisly chief Red-Hand) are set against the valiant Utes; nature is described in rather too much detail (and sometimes in passages merely repeated from earlier works, like the description of the "Butte Herfana" which was lifted bodily from *War Trail*). Even the variations that occur are either borrowed and sensational like the stock Irishman who is also a live scalped victim, or strained and sentimental like the epilogue, in which the praise of motherhood becomes particularly purple: "thine is not a beauty born to blush but for an hour . . . but like the blossom of the citron, seems only fairer by the side of its own fruit!"

We would have to agree with the *Athenaeum* reviewer who complained bitterly about Reid's repetition of character, plot, and setting, and his unwillingness to unravel the complications of his plot as realistically as he described his settings. Clearly, by 1861 Reid has become a hack writer even on the topic that was dearest to his heart. Only two later works with a western setting are worthy of brief note, and then only for the ways in which they break the stereotypes previously developed.

The *Headless Horseman* appeared in 1865, the product of a seasoned novelist who had enjoyed a decade and a half of success as a writer of both adult and juvenile works. Reid at forty-seven was also by this time very nearly bankrupt, having squandered the profits from his books on elegant clothing and elaborate homes. Largely through the promotional efforts of Charles Ollivant, the publication of *Headless Horseman* set Reid on firm financial footing once again. Elizabeth Reid states that "many regard this absorbing romance as Mayne Reid's masterpiece, and in various features it certainly deserves the distinction" (p. 156). The various features include the American setting (as in all Reid's previous adult works except *The Maroon* and *White Gauntlet*), Reid's extravagant variation of Washington Irving's "Legend of Sleepy Hollow"(1820),[11] a slight focus on the question of slavery, and a modification of the Haller-Warfield hero. *Headless Horseman* confirms that as its author became more distanced from his actual adventures he was inclined to build "new" characters and incidents from his previous fictional works and his personal adventures.

The circuitous relationship of author to fiction is unconsciously validated by Mrs. Reid's further remarks that "while writing the 'Headless Horseman', the author—for inspiration as well as diversion—would almost daily mount a fiery black horse, and gallop with headlong speed about the thinly settled country. In these wild rides . . . Mayne Reid in fancy once more roamed over the trackless prairies and virgin forest of the South-Western United States, once more he mingled with the hunter and the mustanger" (p. 156).

Reid's fancy was leading him backwards; except for the nationality of the cast (all the principals are now Americans), echoes of previous works abound in *Headless Horseman*. Briefly sketched, the plot has the family of Woodley Poindexter en route from Louisiana to southwestern Texas to start a new life. The love interest, daughter Louise, is a creature of spirit and passion like her predecessors Isolina de Vargas and Catalina de Cruces. Louise's cousin, Cassius Calhoun, is the villain who seeks both her hand and the land of her father, his uncle. The hero, Maurice Gerald, is a lowly "mustanger" (a kind of proto-cowboy who rounds up wild horses and sells them in the Texas settlements). He thus resembles Carlos of *White Chief* in his desire to make an honest fortune through his work. But he is eventually discovered to be Sir Maurice Gerald, the dispossessed holder of extensive property in Ireland and thus far more of a personal fantasy than his predecessor. Maurice's fortuitous inheritance can clear the mortgage that evil cousin Calhoun holds over Poindexter's head. To prevent this, Calhoun sets out after Maurice, but is confused into stalking and killing Louise's brother Henry by mistake. Henry's decapitated head is abandoned on the prairie; his body is propped on a horse to wander over the countryside as the apparition of the title. Maurice is accused of Henry's murder and brought before Judge Lynch. But through the faultless tracking of Zeb Stump (a fusion character combining the qualities of Bill Garey and Rube Rawlings), justice triumphs.

All this is set in the difficult and challenging landscape of the Far West; as usual Reid is at his best in such nature descriptions as that depicting the desolation following a prairie fire when the few trees have been destroyed: "Their light pinnate foliage has disappeared like flax before the flame. Their existence is only evidenced by charred trunks and blackened boughs" (p. 8). This is the landscape through which the Poindexter party travels, and Reid makes it an organic symbol of their past misfortunes and the personal disasters that lie ahead for them.

Although the issue is peripheral to his plot and purpose of entertainment, Reid is able in 1865 to make more scathing comments on the institution of slavery than appear in his earlier works. The action takes place in 1850 and so Reid can attack the "peculiar institution" more vehemently than before—setting up proslavery arguments as the work of "scribblers in Lucifer's pay" who claim that slavery is a patriarchal institution. "Such arguments—at which a world might weep—have been of late but too often urged. Woe to the man who speaks, and the nation that gives ear to them!" (p. 17). Yet today the significance of such philosophizing has faded to become merely the insight of scholars and social critics who scrutinize the literature of the past. The reader who would enjoy *Headless Horseman* must approach it in the spirit of the *New York Times* review of the novel when it was reissued in 1906, and read it for its "dreamland full of the clatter of hoofs, the popping of Colts, the jingle of spurs, the hissing of words of the villain, and the eager kisses of fair maids" (September 31, p. 634).

Elizabeth Reid may have considered *Headless Horseman* her husband's masterpiece, but Reid himself favored *The Lone Ranche: A Tale of the 'Staked Plain'* (1871).[12] It is certainly quintessential

Reid, perhaps because it was written shortly after his return from
his second visit to America and thus presents a revitalized view of
his favorite topic. The work is also noteworthy for showing the
process of fusion and division we have noted in his creative process.
Lone Ranche begins in Mexico but the scene shifts quickly to Texas,
thus allowing Reid to draw upon his two favorite memories and so
present the kinds of characters and action he depicts best. We
recognize familiar characters and actions: the good Mexican
aristocrat (allied with the American cause) pitted against the
villainous Mexican (allied with a corrupt government and Catholic
Church); the beautiful, dauntless Mexican heroine; the intrepid
backwoodsman; Indian savagery—all are familiar. But permeating
the stereotypes is Reid's political dream of democracy, which he still
assigns to the American people, and his personal fantasy of the
grandeur and beauty of the American land as a refuge and healer.

In *Lone Ranche*, Reid raises two Mexican characters to the
stature of hero and heroine by endowing them with the virtues of
democratic patriotism and love of nature. Colonel Valerian Miranda, who befriends the hero Frank Hamersley and helps him become
the proprietor of a Santa Fe trading caravan, is worthy not only
because his sister is to be the traditional Mexican love-match for the
hero (this was also the case with Narcisso in *Rifle Rangers*) but also
because he is able to live happily under American rule after the
United States takes possession of former Mexican lands. Miranda
realizes that although "the native land had lost its nationality" it is
a "loss the true patriot will never lament, when liberty is the gain"
(II, 291). Miranda's worth is woven into the love plot as well, for at
the concluding marriage ceremony he joins the aristocratic hero and
backwoods character and marries Frank's sister. This is a rare event,
for although the Haller-Warfield-Hamersley character often marries
a "dark" Mexican woman, the reverse is seldom the case.

While Reid's biographical projection of the love of a fearless
Mexican maiden has been rehearsed in such previous works as
White Chief and *War Trail*, Adela Miranda goes beyond that
biographical and sexual dream to enact the fantasy of the American
landscape that also was so much a part of Reid's experience. Adela
is capable of rescuing Frank and his guide Walt Wilder (a sturdy
middle-aged hunter and ex-Texas Ranger: the most believable fusion of Reid's dual backwoods characters) from death on the prairie
through her strength and skill. But she also represents the ideal of
nature as a refuge and escape. She would prefer to remain forever at

the "lone ranche"—a hidden valley oasis far from civilization; as she states, "I've never cared a straw for what the world calls 'society.' I've always liked better to be free from its restraints and conventionalities. Give me Nature for my companion—Nature in her wildest moods. . . . I've never been happier than here in this wilderness home" (II, 59 - 60). Adela's appreciation for the quality of this land raises her to meet Reid's own conception of it and thus makes her marriage to the autobiographical hero one of the most believable and symbolic in the entire canon.

In Reid's earliest works an episodic plot and a digressive tendency to describe whatever is at hand (people, clothes, plants, or animals) alternately vie for predominance. The plots rely upon the typical devices of escapist fiction and a strong degree of sensationalism for their appeal, while the frequent descriptive digressions about surroundings, costumes, and customs satisfy the requirements of a "travel-book." In these works, characters are subservient to both the plot and the digressive tendency, and indeed, there is little integration in the overall work. However, Reid uses his landscapes not only for the local color they provide but also as symbols for philosophical ideals; at the same time, Reid's characters outgrow their functionary roles in the episodic plots and begin to serve as focal points for the "issues" in Reid's writing. His plots remain adventurous, fast paced, and beyond the normal range of credibility, but the interaction of plot, character, and setting allow Reid to use his fiction as a stronger vehicle for the discussion of his ideas and ideals while maintaining his popular appeal. When he is most successful, this combination also creates his best work.

VI *Indians Glorified and Reviled*

In common with many contemporary authors, Reid held two diametrically opposed views about the American Indian and embodied these ideas in specific Indian characters. Either they were like El Sol of *Scalp Hunters*—good, "noble savages" somewhat westernized and really very much like white men—or they were savage and brutal like Chief Red-Hand of *Wild Huntress*, to be hunted and despised. Both of Reid's views have some factual basis derived from his personal observations and from the documents of the time, and yet his own vision was informed by a set of preconceptions about manifest destiny that produced an ambivalence which made it impossible for him to maintain consistency.

Reid's treatment of the warring Navajo horse-Indians of the Plains reflects the attitude pointed out by Roy Harvey Pearce that the conception of the noble savage in America had been denied by the colonial experience, and that Americans were much more prone to exterminate than to civilize their aborigines.[13] However, Reid insists that two distinct species of Indian exist; he often complains of the difference between the literary and (in the 1850's and after) historical Indian of the forest and his more barbaric western brother. In *Scalp Hunters* Reid remarks, "these southern Indians, I knew, possessed none of that cold continence and chivalrous delicacy that characterizes the red men of the 'forest' " (p. 286). And in *War Trail*, trying to accommodate the picture of Indian savagery to that of Cooper's redmen, he comments that the Plains Indians are fierce "uxorious" warriors with no trace of the "ideal type of cold continence, as it has pleased the poet and writer of romance to ascribe to them" (p. 324). With that distinction established, he proceeds to promote the image of the salacious Indian: "No cold ascetic this—no romantic savage, alike celebrated for silence and continence—but a true voluptuary, gay of thought and free of tongue—amorous, salacious, immoral. . . . Women is the constant theme of their conversation, their motive for every act. For these they throw the prairie dice; for these they race their swift mustangs. To win them, they paint in hideous guise; to buy them, they steal horses; to capture them, they go to war!" (p. 337). Less general, and more personal, are the remarks of Seguin, whose career as an Indian bounty hunter began when his eldest daughter Adele was kidnapped by the Navajos: "If you knew the history of this land for the last ten years; its massacres and its murders, its tears and its burnings, its rapes and spoilations, whole provinces depopulated, villages given to the flames, men butchered on their own hearths, women, beautiful women, carried into captivity to satisfy the lust of the desert robber!" (p. 95). The extent to which Reid has colored his narrative becomes clearer when we realize how he has juggled history. A particularly brutal and bloodthirsty cutthroat named Kirker appears in the pages of *Scalp Hunters*. According to Bernard De Voto, a bounty hunter named James Kirker "had collected an elite guard of retired mountain men and the Ishmaels of the plains, the dispossessed Delaware. With this posse of specialists he ranged Chihuahua gathering Apache scalps and was paid fifty dollars per scalp, half price for women and children. (He appears by name in one of the best Wild West novels, Mayne Reid's *Scalp Hunters*, and is really the model of that romance's prettified Gothic hero with the beautiful daughter and the heart of bitter fire.)"[14] Reid used Kirker's band as described by De Voto for the action of his novel. But in order to justify the cruelty and rapacity of the bounty hunters he created an imaginary revenge motif, changed the leader of the band into a wronged father, and relegated the historical model of the leader to a minor speaking part.

The Navajos in *Scalp Hunters* are hunted like wolves, yet they exist side by side with the "noble savages" El Sol and La Luna; moreover, Reid's treatment of Indians in other works varies. When he describes the Seminoles assembled at Fort King before their removal to the western lands, he makes clear he prefers them to their white conquerors: "no eye could have looked upon them without acknowledging the superiority of the savage" (*Oçeola*, p. 133). His ambivalence extends even to the horse-Indians, whom he glorifies in *Despard the Sportsman* as "the plumed and painted horsemen of the plains [who] almost rival in interest the steel clad heroes of the medieval times" (p. 16). The key word is "interest": Reid's adventurous Indians are used melodramatically to provide exoticism. In his attempts to exonerate these Indians he sometimes shifts the blame for evil deeds to those worse villains, the Mexicans, who often form pseudowar parties to frighten the local population by committing barbarous acts for which the Indians are blamed. The reader can usually guess that if a particularly vile deed has been done it has been done in masquerades of this kind—sometimes even by white villains. The idea seems to follow Cooper: a Red Indian may be forgiven for committing a savage act which is in his "nature," but there is no forgiveness for a similar act committed by a white man.

Almost all of Reid's Indians are flat figures of villainy or virtue. Reid telegraphs the presence of a villainous Indian as he describes Red-Hand, chief of the Arapahoes, whose totem appears on his shield to remind the hero of the "noted chief of the name, famed for his hostility to the trappers . . . a savage who is said to take delight in torturing his captives. . . . Can it be that fiend—the Red-Hand of the Arapahoes? The appearance of the man confirms my suspicion. A body, tall, angular, and ill-shaped, scarred with cicatrized wounds . . . a face seamed with the traces of evil passion; eyes deep sunken in their sockets, and sparkling like coal's fire—an

aspect more fiendish than human" (*Wild Huntress*, pp. 250 - 51).
Red-Hand's bloody deeds are as advertised. On the other hand, Indians may be virtuous, as is Wakara of *Wild Huntress*, when they are necessary to a plot rescue. Wakara, a highly idealized Ute war chief, helps the heroes rescue Marian Holt from the dastardly Arapahoes under Chief Red-Hand. And so the action becomes a confrontation between tribes, the Utes serving the white man's cause.

Thus in his trans-Mississippi adventures Reid employs primarily stock Indian figures for purposes of depicting action; arousing fear; stimulating sexual appetites and racial strife: all leading to a saleable exoticism. His inability to take a consistent moral position was no doubt dictated by the complexity of the problem. For Reid, whose whole philosophy was based on the premises of radicalism and escapism, would be unable to resolve the dilemma of what to do with a noble savage one is committed to destroy. Roy Harvey Pearce comments that "at bottom, primitivistic thinking . . . was always radical" yet weak because it was "tied to a simplistic fantasy" (pp. 146 - 47). Reid's tales futher reinforce Pearce's thesis that where Indians are depicted in literature the "interest is not in the Indian as Indian, but in the Indian as vehicle for understanding the white man, in the savage defined in terms of the ideas and needs of civilized life" (p. 202). Some of Reid's characters (notably Rube and Seguin) become Indian-haters who have been "savagized" by their contact with the natives; eventually they are so removed from civilization and its responsibilities that they do not even notice that they have become the mirror image of the enemy: hunters for scalps. The Indian-hater who returns without guilt to civilization (as Seguin does) may be seen as a symbol of the victory of America over its Indians, from whom it has taken both land and life. Although Reid is only dimly aware of this, it is evident in his works. Reid would prefer to think there can be a pragmatic "civilized" solution to the Indian question, one he proposes in *Hunter's Feast:* "It is predicted that in a few years the race [buffalo] will become extinct. The same has often been said of the Indian. Believe me, there is not the slightest danger of such a destiny for the Indian; his race is not to become extinct; it will be on the earth as long as that of either black or white. Civilization . . . will preserve the race of the red man yet to multiply. Civilization, too, may preserve the buffalo" (p. 295). Both the Indian and the buffalo have survived extinction—the Indian largely through adaptation. Reid suggested this in a note to the first edition of *Scalp Hunters*, stating, "I do not believe that any race possessing the organization of manhood so perfect as they, can be shuffled from the earth's surface so easily." Reid continues to discuss the right of the colonists to take the lands of the Indian hunters in the name of progress, for "no handful of men have the right to hold from the great body of mankind a valuable portion of the earth's surface without *using* it" and if other tribes would profit from the example of the Five Tribes and prosper by farming "instead of their decreasing, we will find them increasing, and forming, at no distant day, an important amalgam with the Anglo-American race" (pp. 292 - 94).

Reid's ambivalences are clear. Much as he extolled or embellished exciting adventure, he yet believed the world must progress from the hunter to the agriculturalist. Because of his sincere belief in the brotherhood of man, implicit in the last statement quoted, he refused to face the question of whether the Indian would have preferred to retain both his lands and his cultural-racial identity, a question many since his day have refused to face.

The discussion of Indians, begun in *Scalp Hunters* and continued through *White Chief, War Trail,* and *Wild Huntress*, reaches its fullest, most favorable and humane treatment in *Oçeola* (1859). In the other works the Indians are intermediaries in the plot and incidental to the theme, but in *Oçeola* the Indian hero shares center stage in the dual plots: one the standard sensational melodrama, the other firmly founded on historical fact. In order to gain a willing ear for his social or political "message," Reid often develops his melodramatic plots deliberately. Hence the two plot strands of *Oçeola.* The first deals with the love affair of the gentleman-hero, George Randolph, and Maümee, Osceola's sister. This sentimental-sensational-gothic story, full of misunderstandings, mistaken identities, and unresolved mysteries, and capped by the wild incantations of the Indian sorceress Haj-Ewa (who somehow manipulates events in favor of the hero), was aimed at popular taste. It is combined, however, with an historical narrative of the Seminole chief Osceola and his valiant attempts to save his people and their homeland. In this history Reid uses actual events and persons, such as Dade's Massacre of December 25, 1835, when Indian Commissioner Wiley Thompson was murdered by Osceola's band. He further attempts to give the historical plot verisimilitude by quoting official reports of expeditions that visited the scene of the battle. Fully aware of the injustice of the Seminole War, Reid tries to erase

the reputation for savagery from the Indians of *Oçeola*. Having established the white man's persecution of the Seminoles, he suggests
that stories of Indian torture have been greatly exaggerated, "and
ferocity can be charged with as much justice against white skin as
against red skin. Had the Indian written the story of border warfare,
the world might have modified its belief in their so called cruelty"
(p. 62). Always he is working toward a goal of closing the gap
between men, and establishing their essential kinship. To this end,
Reid develops Osceola as a tragic hero, whose personal and tribal
tragedy serves Reid very well in the promotion of his own theses
about government, freedom, and racial equality.

It would be gratifying to be able to speak of Osceola as a fully
realized Indian character, stalking heroically and stoically toward
his historical doom. Unfortunately, he is not. Although he is based
on an historical person, he must figure in Reid's melodramatic story
and to effect this Reid makes his Osceola a puppet of his own
idealization. Osceola becomes a white man's Redman; he is always
ready to leave his tribal councils for a last-minute rescue of the
whites; his manners would do justice to the royal court; he speaks a
lofty philosophical prose. And this figure, resigned to his doom, a
creature of Reid's imagination, is set in motion performing the daring and even bloodthirsty deeds of the historical Osceola. The dis-
crepancy is too great, and we almost long for the colorful
Comanches of *War Trail*, who were not believable either, but at
least had no philosophical burdens to hamper them.

As in several of his other novels, Reid's plot supports the idea of
an eventual solution to the problem of racial strife through inter-
marriage. Reid depicts Osceola as a halfbreed whose father was an
English trader named Powell. This might be suspect on the grounds
that Reid was trying to make the romance between the heroine
Virginia Randolph and the Indian hero more palatable. But
although most modern authorities agree that Powell was actually
Osceola's stepfather, Reid drew upon nineteenth-century accounts
for his facts; he repeatedly quotes from a "faithful history" which
he does not identify.[15] He speaks of Osceola's mixed blood in admiring terms: "the Caucasian blood had tamed down the
prominence of Indian features to a perfect regularity, without rob-
bing them of their heroic grandeur of expression" (p. 51). Yet Reid
observes his customary double standard (broken only by *White
Squaw*), for George Randolph, himself a descendant of Pocahontas,
is perfectly willing to mix his blood with that of Osceola's sister

Maümee, and states the historical precedent of Rolfe for so doing. Yet he is aghast at the thought of his sister Virginia becoming Osceola's wife: "I was slave to a belief in the monstrous anomaly that where the blood is mingled from the other side—where the woman is white and the man red—the union becomes a mésalliance, a disgrace. . . . To believe my sister in love with an Indian, would be to regard her as lost—fallen! No matter how high in rank among his own people—no matter how brave—how accomplished he might be—no matter if it were Osceola himself!" (p. 270). Although we cannot assume the voice of George Randolph to be that of Mayne Reid, the attitudes expressed seem to represent two qualities of Reid's work: English and American, romantic and realistic. Here he treats miscegenation almost as an earlier English gothic novelist would have treated incest, practically revelling in the thrill and horror of it. Yet this is also an accurate report of American social mores. Reid records accurately what he knew of American society; the white man may mingle as he pleases, but not the white woman. This was reality—the condition as it existed—and Reid reports it as fact. Yet he also holds to his passionate romantic vision of America as the melting pot—an idea that was to inform Europe well into the twentieth century. Reid's disparity between realism and romance, between radicalism and fantasy, is too great for a true synthesis ever to be achieved.

VII *Slavery as a Subtext*

Given the escapist quality of Mayne Reid's romances and their predominant setting in the New World, it might seem surprising that he would deal with disturbing social issues. Yet his life, which provided both fact and fantasy for his work, made the issue of human freedom pervasive in his romances. While radical political ideas appear in nearly all his works, the overwhelming emphasis is on the abolition of slavery—before, during, and after the American Civil War. The subject is treated most fully in *The Quadroon* (1856), a close examination of which will highlight the most important of his views on the racial question. As always, Reid uses a melodramatic plot structure as a vehicle. Here the young hero Edward Rutherford (again a first-person narrator) is adrift in New Orleans after having arrived in "January, 18—".[16] Deciding to go upstream to St. Louis to avoid the yellow-fever season, Rutherford books passage on a steamboat which explodes during a race with a rival vessel; he awakens after the disaster to find himself at the plantation of a lovely fellow-passenger, Eugénie Besançon. Eugénie's gratitude to Edward for having saved her from the river rapidly ripens into love. But Edward has fallen madly in love with Eugénie's beautiful quadroon maid, Aurore. The gracious Creole hostess is in dire danger from the evil lawyer Gayarre, who holds the plantation mortgage and also wants to possess Aurore. In due course, Gayarre forecloses, Eugénie flees to a convent, and Rutherford determines to use his last dollar to purchase the freedom of Aurore when she goes on the block at the slave market. When his letter of credit from England does not arrive in time he accepts the aid of a handsome Creole youth, Eugene de Hauteville (really Eugénie in disguise), but Eugene's $3,000 is not enough to purchase Aurore and the villain's agent wins her at $3,500. So Edward and "Eugene" kidnap Aurore from Gayarre's plantation; chased by hounds and brought to bay, they are saved from lynching only by the timely arrival of a posse of respectable planters. Shortly thereafter a courtroom scene reveals that Gayarre had stolen Aurore's manumission papers, whereupon "Eugene" accuses Gayarre of embezzling from the Besançon estate and reveals herself as Eugénie. Justice is meted out to all and sundry, the beautiful Eugénie (another of Reid's strong-willed women) does not yield to despair over her unfortunate love, but uses her energy "to pluck the fatal arrow from her heart" (p. 377). The reader presumes that Edward and Aurore live happily ever after, although a careful reading of the denouement reveals some equivocation in the admonition, "you, reader, will scarce be curious to lift the curtain that veils the tranquil after-life of myself and my beautiful Quadroon" (p. 379). However, in spite of this hedging (perhaps for the benefit of his American audience), Reid's position is clear throughout the novel; he sees no impediment to the match in the mixed blood of his heroine.

The book was reviewed in the *Athenaeum* solely on the plot level; a brief description of the events is given, together with a comment about the novel's similarity to the melodramas commonly presented at Astley's Amphitheatre. Aside from some favorable remarks on Reid's brilliant handling of the nature descriptions, which have the "freshness of out-of-door nature upon them, that indescribable air of reality which is not to be obtained at second hand," the reviewer sees nothing in the book beyond "mere amusement . . . a book to read and not to sleep over" (August 16, 1856,

p. 1019). Perhaps it is with the advantage of hindsight that a twentieth-century reader, while not claiming any more literary significance for the novel than was acknowledged in the review, can see in its pages hints of Reid's understanding of America's most severe problem: the institution of slavery and the relations between the races.

Reid was certain that there could be no solution to the general problem of racial relations so long as slavery existed. But he is careful in his "Preface" to *The Quadroon* to disclaim any "intention." The book, he states, "has been written, neither to aid the abolitionist, nor glorify the planter. The author does not believe that by such means he could benefit the slave, else he would not fear to avow it. On the other hand, he is too true a Republican, to be the instrument that would add one drop to the 'bad blood' which, unfortunately for the cause of human freedom, has already arisen between 'North' and 'South.' No: he will be the last man to aid European despots in this, their dearest wish and desperate hope." Precisely because he has not taken any avowed position, remaining true to the demands of his melodrama, the evils of slavery come through far more strongly than they might have had he taken a more vehement and propagandistic stance.

There are two familiar sensational aspects in the story of *The Quadroon*. The first, of course, is the possibility of the nearly white girl (frequently a daughter of the house) being sold "down the river" under financial pressure. A factual situation of this sort was reported by Harriet Martineau and a similar incident occurs in Longfellow's poem "The Quadroon Girl" (1853). The second aspect, that of a liaison between a white man and a woman of color, was one which captured the imagination of the British public. Most treatments of the subject, however, were less honest than Reid's. Authors had various options; they could kill off the heroine and thus prevent the match, or use the changeling plot device wherein the story is arranged so that none of the principal "good" characters turns out to be of mixed blood after all.

While Reid uses sensationalism and melodrama in *The Quadroon* to reinforce the values of freedom, he is not always successful in fighting the stereotypes of the time. He has a rather naïve view of Negro slaves who express admiration for "Massa Edward [who is] good to brack folk" (p. 214). His depiction of the "devil's douche" water torture seems gratuitous and sensational, merely a device to enable Edward Rutherford to be as heroic as possible when he

rescues the suffering slave. Yet the hope of freedom inspires the
black man to deeds of valor incongruous with his slavish condition.
When the runaway slave Gabriel assists Edward Rutherford to escape, the reader is told that "the spirit of liberty alone could have
inspired him with that courage" (p. 177). On the other hand, while
Reid's graphic description of the slave mart at which Aurore is auc-
tioned is very powerful, it is weakened in part by the melodramatic
stance of the narrator who sees the sufferings of all the slaves, but
thinks only of himself and Aurore. And Reid, the English radical,
often uses the pages of *The Quadroon* for invidious comparisons of
English and American "slavery," stating for example that "this
black man is a slave, and there are three million of his race in the
same condition. But this thought is accompanied by the reflection
that the same broad land is trodden by twenty millions of free and
sovereign men. Three millions of slaves to twenty millions of
masters. In mine own land the proportion is exactly reversed! The
truth may be obscure. For all that, I dare say there are some who
will understand it" (p. 40).

As a matter of fact, Reid's most scathing denunciations of slavery
occur in *The Maroon* (1862) for reasons which are not hard to ascertain. When an author's characters operate in a particular milieu
where an institution is flourishing and where a goodly number of
his readers also reside, it is difficult to advocate reform and still
maintain sympathy for the principal characters. In *The Quadroon*,
Eugénie is clearly a sympathetic character, yet she is mistress of a
plantation containing many slaves. And while Reid deplores the
system, he cannot preach too strongly, lest he destroy the reader's
rapport with Eugénie and hence with Edward and Aurore as well.
This difficulty is even more apparent in *Oçeola*, where the
necessities of the plot require Reid to present a sympathetic description of slave-quarter life because the white hero is the heir to a
Florida plantation.

It was far easier to be indignant about slavery in a locale where it
no longer legally existed, which may account for the more vehement denunciations found in *The Maroon*. Again the method is
melodrama, but here the characters who make the case for equality
exist at all levels of society. For the heroine, Kate Vaughan, is the
daughter of a wealthy Jamaican planter who has concealed her mixed blood in order that she may marry and inherit the estate; she is
not of the servant class as was Aurore. And Kate, even when her
"tainted blood" is revealed, is allowed to marry the enlightened
English hero Herbert. While performing the requisite Reid adven-

tures—living off the land and unravelling mysteries—Herbert functions as a mediator between races and castes. He qualifies because of his "English heart—still uncorrupted by vile prejudices of caste and colour" (I, 269). In this milieu blacks may be princes like Cingües, who has come to Jamaica in search of his sister Yola, who was kidnapped into slavery; they may be leaders of the local people like Cubina, a veritable Robin Hood of the Maroons and Kate's half-brother; or (to serve the gothic elements of the tale) they may be evil like the hunchback medicine man Chakra, whose vileness is explained in part because of his practice of obeah (which Reid depicts as a kind of sensationalized black Catholicism). The virtue of the white characters is closely related to their position on slavery, and even Reid's anti-Semitic attacks on the overseer Jacob Jessuron are always qualified by Jessuron's being cast as himself a victim of discrimination resembling the injustice of slavery through "twenty centuries of outrage, calumny, and wrong—housed in low haunts—pillaged and persecuted—oft driven to desperation" (I, 83).

The plot of *The Maroon* provides Reid the opportunity to attack the "infamous black code of Jamaica" (I, 162), which included the provision that anyone with one-eighth or more black blood could not inherit property. Reid also insists on the destruction of morality inherent in slavery and so evident in the persons of mixed blood to be seen everywhere in Jamaica. The novel shows Reid's wide reading in the history of oppressed peoples, and his attention to etymological detail. The title does not mean "to abandon on a desert island" (its more typical verbal meaning and that which William Gilmore Simms used in his 1855 title *The Maroon*). Instead Reid develops the nominative meaning of "hog hunters" given to the Jamaican fugitive slaves of the Spaniards who had taken to the hills and defended their freedom against the English since 1650. Reid abrogates biography to history to the extent that his usual first-person narrator appears only in the introductory chapter to provide a description of the locale and set the theme to be superimposed on the gothic melodrama to follow. The sight of the now-deserted port of Montego Bay, once the center of the slave trade, reminds the narrator of the "Maroons . . . those brave black men, who, for 200 years, maintained their independence against the whole white population of the island" (I, 5). He then finds one of their descendants, who proceeds to tell him the inset story that comprises the narrative.

Certainly for Reid the presence of freedom is the one thing required to bring about equality. He demonstrates this clearly in *The Maroon*, whose title characters are compared to the "Mountain Men" of the American West, legendary symbols of pure freedom. These maroons call themselves mountain men, they speak like mountain men, and act like them as well. And so once more Reid reaches for an American frame of reference to make a philosophical point. But Reid's radicalism was grounded in reality; he was well aware of the economic forces behind slavery and consequently the zenith of villainy was engagement in the slave trade itself. He makes the point with typical hyperbole when he describes the fate of a slaver who, captured on an African expedition, was caught, chopped, "cooked and eaten at the grand national feast. . . . One might have felt sympathy for the unfortunate wretch had he been anything else than a dealer in human flesh" (III, 351).

This issue also is touched on in many of Reid's juvenile titles, where although adventure is always foremost, abolitionism is included along with the other educational messages. For example, in *The Forest Exiles* (1854), Reid follows his common practice of turning his knowledge of botany toward political ends. Discussing the importance of palm oil as an article of commerce, he remarks that "the native princes, finding that it is more profitable than slave-selling, have in many parts given up the last-named atrocious commerce, and have taken to gathering palm-oil. If a palm tree can effect what has baffled the skill of the combined philanthropists and powers of Europe, then indeed, we shall say 'all honour to the noble palm' " (p. 107).

Reid tries very hard to break through stereotypical patterns when depicting Negro characters; once again his accuracy interferes, for he is drawing persons whose very existence was circumscribed by limitations he could not transcend. Reid, like most men of his generation, was hampered by beliefs in the childlike nature of the black man, common both in the traditions of literature and in the life he had observed in the American South, where clever blacks soon learned to adopt a servile pleasantness in order to survive. Only in recent years have Americans become aware of the institutional and psychological complexitities of involuntary servitude. Consequently, Reid's understanding of the universal humanity of his Negro characters can be seen as advanced, considering the lack of knowledge available to him. One example of this occurs when the young slave Jupiter, finding Charles Clancy, the wounded and abandoned hero of *Death Shot* (1873), ponders whether to risk his own life by rescuing the wounded man: "Slave, mulatto, nigger, as they call me, I'll show them that under a coloured skin can be gratitude, as much as under a white one—may be more" (p. 152). Also in *Death Shot* the faithful black servant Blue Bill gambles all to attain justice. Fighting a legal code that denies his manhood by ruling his own testimony inadmissible in a court of law, he so manipulates matters that he can present his evidence second-hand (with the help of the intrepid white trapper Simeon Woodley) even though he knows his life may be forfeit if his master should discover what he has done. After a touching conference with his wife, Phoebe, in which Reid explores the reprehensible position of the chattel slave, the two agree that justice must be served, regardless of the consequences. "And then their two black faces come in contact, as also their bosoms; both beating with a humanity that might shame whiter skins" (p. 94). In common with most men, Reid can solve the problem of injustice and inhumanity better in the abstract than in the concrete. He very early took an anti-slavery position, and maintained it consistently except when forced by the exigencies of his plots to equivocate somewhat. Since he often was describing life in southern and southwestern America at a time when slavery was very much a part of the social and political scene he could not change this reality without being untrue to the factual basis underlying his most improbable stories. His solution was frequently to make his "good" characters "good" slaveholders, aware of slavery's evils, but prisoners of the system. Moreover, in his treatment of the minority races of America he clearly demonstrates his conception of the essential brotherhood of man, as well as his dream for the ultimate freedom of all men.

VIII   *English History as a Radical Text*

Mayne Reid's rebellious nature and hatred of authority provide a constant strand throughout his life and work. He planned great deeds of espionage in the service of the Hungarian revolutionary Louis Kossuth, and although they failed to materialize, he later made them the basis for his fiction. His unpublished correspondence gives evidence of the many speeches he made in defense of the Hungarian patriot, and Mrs. Reid reports that her husband planned to smuggle Kossuth out of England disguised as his servant. Improbable as this may sound, it is verified in the autobiography of Henry Vizetelly, who recounts Reid's attempts to

obtain false passports "to enable him to carry out a mad scheme he
had devised of going to Milan in company of Kossuth—the pair of
them being of course duly disguised—to assist in a rising against the
Austrians which had just taken place.[17] Reid fictionalized these
matters in *The Child Wife* (1868), an extremely autobiographical
novel whose hero, "Captain Maynard—he who led the forlorn hope
at C————" (p. 45), leaves America after the Mexican War with his
friend "Count Rosenvelt" (Friedrich Hecker) en route to the European revolutions and who later befriends Louis Kossuth in a series
of cloak-and-dagger intrigues. Although not the first of Reid's works
to focus on his radical political beliefs, *Child Wife* is a crucial one.
In spite of its title, the book is really about the adult husband as he
looks backward over a fifteen-year time span. *Child Wife* is a formula Reid romance; its love story is a nearly exact recapitulation of
the Reid-Hyde romance and the adventures are drawn from Reid's
own escapades, real and imaginary. The book also allows him to
vent his spleen on the aristocracy in chapters with titles like "The
Conspiracy of Crowns." But most important, *Child Wife*, written
just past the midpoint of his career, validates both Reid's consistent
radicalism and his pervasive egocentricity. For example, we shall
never know how much fact and fiction are blended in this scene
when Reid-Maynard, about to set off for the European revolutions,
is given a wildly enthusiastic send-off in New York City: "It had not
much to do with the man. Only that he was the representative of a
principle—a cause for which most of them had fought and bled,
and many intended fighting, and, if need be, bleeding again. He
was their chosen chief, advancing toward the van, flinging himself
forward into the post of peril—for man's and liberty's sake, risking
the chain and the halter. For this was he the recipient of such
honors. . . . 'It is worth while to be true to the people,' said
Maynard, his breast glowing with proud triumph . . . as he listened
to the distant cheers sent after him across the widening water" (pp.
111 - 12).

The autobiographical thread is pervasive in both plot and
theme—sometimes with an unconscious psychological significance
such as this quotation from a purported review of the hero's first
novel: "Of Captain Maynard it may be said what Byron wrote of
Bonaparte, —'And quiet to quick bosoms is a hell' " (p. 244). Even
thus distanced—as an imaginary review of an imaginary book—the
quotation is extraordinarily revealing. Reid the frustrated man of
action, the romantic defender of Byron, the rebellious radical with

authoritarian inclinations, was certainly a man of quick bosom most of whose later life was spent in the hellish quiet that produced a fiction to serve as a surrogate for that which life had denied him. Yet the quotation is not really imaginary. In her *Memoir*, Elizabeth Reid quotes an enlightening variation taken from the *Observer* of April 7, 1850: "Of Captain Mayne Reid may be said, according to his own analysis of himself, what Byron wrote of Bonaparte . . ." (p. 142). This transcription of fact into fiction and then into biography is representative of the continual intermingling that both makes biographical accuracy impossible and demonstrates the dependence of Reid's works on his life.

The autobiographical element is more subtle in Reid's other two politically focused works—both historical novels. Reid rarely wrote historical fiction: his choice of period indicates how seriously he took his subject. Both *White Gauntlet* (1864) and *No Quarter!* (1888, but serialized in the *Boys' Illustrated Newspaper*, 1881 - 82) are set in pre-Cromwellian England and both are vitriolic attacks on the monarchy not only of the seventeenth but also of the nineteenth century. Both works are true to Reid's established pattern of melodrama: they contain the dual lovers, battles, and death-defying escapes that we remember from his American adventure tales. But no Mexican was ever so vile as are the minions of Charles Stuart. And although Reid admiringly describes the English countryside, politics takes center stage.

White Gauntlet takes place in Buckinghamshire, where Reid was living at the time he wrote the book. Its heroine, Marion Wade, daughter of Sir Marmaduke—an aristocratic Parliamentarian—is even more enlightened politically than her father: "more than once had her counsel guided his wavering resolves; influencing him . . . to that determination . . . to declare for the Parliament and people" (p. 233). Marion is a direct descendant of Reid's Mexican heroines and is not afraid to dare all in her romance with the mysterious "black horseman" Henry Holtspur, whose dual purpose in life is to arouse the local peasantry to the Parliamentary cause and to win fair Marion. Holtspur is Reid set back nearly two hundred years—"a man of ready determination" resulting from living "under the shadows of primeval American forests" (p. 270). Traces of the American frontier anachronistically surround him; his years in the American colonies are represented by his dress—a strange combination of doublet, beaver, and buckskin—and his mysteriously mute Indian servant Oriole.

Holtspur again is Reid's fantasy-figure Haller reincarnated. He is the spokesman for the cause of liberty around the countryside, and when he rises to address a secret gathering of Puritans "the sounds became hushed, but only for an instant. Then arose something more than a murmur of applause—amidst which could be heard . . . the sobriquet by which to most of them he was better known" (p. 193). The sobriquet is the *black horseman* (always italicized) and we are reminded of the many sable steeds that have carried and will bear Reid's heroes to their thrilling destinies. Holtspur's speech reflects Reid's sentiments: "The time is come, not only for the dethronement of a tyrant, but for establishing in dear old England the only form of government that is not a mockery of common sense—the only one upon which Liberty may rely—the Republic" (p. 194). Reid's authorial asides reinforce both his text and his reliance upon his American experience as he comments that had Holtspur "lived in the present time . . . he would have recognized—as I do—in what others call the failure of republican institutions [i.e., the Civil War], their proudest triumph. He would have seen thirty millions of men, comparatively with the rest of their race, transformed into giants, by the influence of less than a century of republican training! He would have seen them divided into two parties—warring against each other like Titans of the olden time; and seeing this, he could have come to no other conclusion, than that, united, these thirty millions of republican people would have been a match for the whole monarchical world!" (p. 195).

Reid's excesses, not the least of which are his alliterations (Star Chamber and the Court of High Commission are "these truculent tools of tyranny" and Charles is the "royal reptile"), elicited the comment of the *Reader* that "it must be a good cause indeed that such advocacy . . . cannot injure" (November 19, 1864, p. 635). But *White Gauntlet* is relatively moderate, compared with Reid's last work, *No Quarter!*, which is characterized by an extremely strained effort to draw similarities between the 1640's and 1880. The motto of Reid's hero, "he who is not a Republican must either have a bad head or a bad heart," is borne out by the action.

One man of good head and heart is Ambrose Powell, father of the two lovely sisters whose favors are to be sought by heroes and villains alike. Powell's studies have "conducted him to a belief—a full, firm conviction—in the superiority of republican institutions; as it must all whose minds are as God made or intended them, and not perverted by prejudice or corrupted by false teachings" (I, 107).

Powell's elder daughter Sabrina is courted by the chivalric, aristocratic, republican Sir Richard Walwyn, while her sister Vaga is sought by the two courtly Trevor cousins, Reginald and Eustace. Influenced by Walwyn, Eustace Trevor is soon converted to republican principles and thus can win the heart of Vaga. Reginald Trevor's reformation is delayed till the end of the book, when he opportunely redeems himself by rescuing the Roundhead forces from the archvillain Prince Rupert.

But the plot is inconsequential. Reid's historical accuracy remains constant and the opposing forces conquer and reconquer Bristol, Gloucester, and Monmouth, with the population always siding with the Republicans. What we note here is Reid's diminishing focus on the melodrama and his insistence upon the parallels between past and present. England, he insists, is no wiser in the present than it was in the reign of Charles Stuart; even the recent "Liberal victory" cannot offset Parliament's "sanctioning and endorsing deeds that have brought a blight on the nation's name, and a cloud over its character, that will take centuries to clear off" (I, 162 - 63). Nor can the wars of modern times be compared with the glories of the past, for it is ". . . indeed difficult to point out any war in which Great Britain has been engaged since not undertaken for the propping up of vile despotisms, or for selfish purposes equally vile, to the very latest of them—Zululand and Afghanistan, *videlicet*" (III, 17).

What then is the recourse for a liberal and independent spirit? With *No Quarter!* Reid returns full circle; his sentiments direct his characters on a course of action that was at once his political belief and his romantic fantasy. The solution is foreshadowed in the first volume: "From this standard [republicanism] rather has there been retrogression since that glorious decade when it was the Government of England. At the Restoration its spirit, with many of its staunchest upholders, took flight to a land beyond the Atlantic, there to breathe freely, live a new life, call into existence and nourish a new nation, ere long destined to dictate the policy and control the action of every other, in the civilized world" (I, 242).

Thus the virtuous characters of Reid's last fiction will escape to the land where he believed freedom and justice prevailed. At the close of the book we learn that "they went away, to become part of that people, the freest, most powerful, and most prosperous on earth" (III, 261). And thus the ring of romance closes with adventure, exoticism, and radical thought all most at home in the new world for which Reid yearned from first to last.

CHAPTER 3

Discovering the Juvenile Market

MOST of Mayne Reid's works were published originally in expensive three-volume editions later to be reissued as railway novels, dime novels, and children's editions. Through the course of time, he has come to be thought of as a children's author although such works as *The Scalp Hunters* (1851)—listed as a "juvenile" best-seller by Richard D. Altick—were not intended for a children's audience.[1] Because of Reid's importance as a children's author, this chapter will establish the tradition of the English juvenile adventure tale in which he plays such an important part. It also will consider his importance in that tradition on two levels: the "primary" level of pure adventure found in those books he wrote specifically for children, and the "secondary" level of the more sophisticated political and social attitudes present in the "adult" romances that were, in time, to become "children's books." This is a rather complex problem, for Reid's work falls into two categories: books whose content, tone, and style were addressed to children—often works of adventure in the tradition of *Robinson Crusoe*—and adventure tales full of sex and violence, directed to adults but eventually read (sometimes in abridged versions) by children.

Children have always appropriated adult books and made them their own. This is particularly true of such tales of adventure as *Robinson Crusoe* and *Gulliver's Travels*, perhaps the only eighteenth-century novels still read by a general audience, and yet never really intended for children. On the other hand, Robert Louis Stevenson and Lewis Carroll, who wrote for children, were and are enjoyed by adults as well. The reciprocity of interest that enabled these writers to bridge the generations may be explained in part by Harvey Darton's comment on Stevenson, perhaps the last and greatest in the nineteenth-century canon of writers of adventure tales: "That was the secret, not that boys delighted in tales meant for men, like *Robinson Crusoe* and *Midshipman Easy*, but that men—Victorian men—were eager for tales meant for boys, like *Treasure Island*.[2] Mayne Reid himself began his career writing "novels" for an adult audience; many of these books later became very popular with boys, as well as those works (about half his canon) that were expressly directed to children. Reid was not pleased at the turn his career took in mid-century, for children's literature was not then considered the serious art form it has become in the twentieth century. Reid wrote to Charles Kent of the London *Sun* in July 1856, "Ah! my dear friend, those boys [sic] books of which you say such good things have been my *sad mistake* I fear. They have procrastinated—perhaps ruined the literary fame I at one time hoped to have reached."[3] But the boys' books sold, and Reid received not only money but adulation from this new audience.

Before the seventeenth century there were few children's books that offered their readers pleasure rather than moral instruction. But no doubt the children who read Bunyan's *Pilgrim's Progress* (1684) ignored much of the allegory and concentrated on the adventures, for action has always been important for holding the attention of young readers. Clearly, one of the first descendants of *Pilgrim's Progress* was *Robinson Crusoe*, as it in turn was the ancestor of the nineteenth-century adventure tales.

I *The English Juvenile Adventure Tale*

Robinson Crusoe presents a mixture of the real and the fabulous, and Crusoe is credible because of Defoe's meticulous reporting, which appeals to young and old alike. In addition, children can identify with the hero because their own maturation experiences are analagous to Crusoe's building a new life on the island. Crusoe's industry appeals to them, for example, because children are not blasé and tired—stranded on a desert island they would want to work and create, not to lead the life of indolence that would appeal to an adult weary with the world. The qualities of Defoe's work give it an appeal to all who have a pioneer spirit, survival instinct, and perhaps most of all, curiosity. *Robinson Crusoe* depicts an unknown world wherein isolate man can create both a physical and emotional life for himself.

The viability of *Robinson Crusoe* is attested to by the host of "Robinsonnades" that followed the original. This convenient term was coined by French bibliographers to describe the imitations produced after the model of *Robinson Crusoe*. (For an analysis of the variations within the type, see Darton, pp. 113 - 31). From St. Pierre's *Paul et Virginie* (1788), through Wyss's *Swiss Family Robinson* (1813), Marryat's *Masterman Ready* (1814), Mayne Reid's *The Desert Home* (1851), and R. M. Ballantyne's *The Coral Island* (1857)—as well as such modern works as Richard Hughes's *The Innocent Voyage* (1929) and William Golding's *Lord of the Flies* (1954)—the variety is endless. These "Robinsonnades" are part of an archetypal adventure-tale tradition which also finds expression in such works as Scott's historical adventures and Cooper's hunter and Red-Indian fiction, as well as the many imitations and combinations that proliferate in the period. A specific "island" locale is not essential, only the island spirit. Cooper's heroes, for example, often must live off the land and fend for themselves.

The adventure tales undoubtedly enabled English youths to live an imaginative, romantic existence denied them by the strictures of real life. By the mid-nineteenth century, in the words of Geoffrey Trease, the "terrible twins, Morality and Instruction," had been clothed or camouflaged "in the dress of castaways, fur-traders, or boys of Rugby School."[4] The future builders of the empire were thus able to enlarge their perspective geographically as well as historically—to dream of real yet distant lands awaiting exploration. The tales of adventure that laid the foundation for these dreams contributed to the spread of English culture and influence throughout the world. It was a circular process: the writers wrote of exotic and enticing lands, and when they grew to manhood the youthful audience accepted the challenge to adventure and empire-building.

Several characteristics are common to the adventure story so favored by English children. A moral or didactic purpose had been present in juvenile literature from its inception; with these tales of high adventure the lesson is no longer merely an instruction for individual behavior; it has a wider scope, becoming a kind of national instruction about a vastly widened world of which the children might otherwise not be aware. This interest in distant places is an example of how the society and its juvenile literature complemented one another. The English, with their history of colonial conquest and seafaring adventure, would naturally write about it in books for children at a time when both children and national expansion were assuming greater importance. The sheer numbers of child-readers were increased by a series of education bills. The

Education Grant rose from £20,000 in 1832 to £663,400 in 1858. Other factors were the 1840 Grammar School Act and the appointment of a Minister for Educational Affairs in 1856. Perhaps the most important legislation of the period was the Elementary Education Act of 1870 which moved toward compulsory attendance and free education for children between the ages of five and ten. The trend to compulsory education was accelerated by the Act of 1876, which made parents legally responsible for seeing that children received adequate instruction in reading, writing, and arithmetic. At the same time, an increasingly prosperous English economy could afford to pamper the burgeoning literacy of its children by creating a special brand of literature for them, especially in the hope that children who read about the dauntless exploits of Englishmen abroad would grow up to emulate these heroes.

Mayne Reid, often described as "the British Cooper," really belongs more in the Defoe tradition. A "Memoir" by Richard Henry Stoddard frequently printed as an introduction to various later editions of the Reid novels states this idea succinctly: "What Defoe is in *Robinson Crusoe*—the realistic idyl of island solitude—that, in his romantic stories of wilderness life, is his great scholar, Captain Mayne Reid." A continuum can be constructed with Defoe at one end, representing a pragmatic philosophy presented in a journalistic and rather mundane style; Cooper at the other end: more romantic, aristocratic, and abstract. Cooper's descriptive details are often static, which accounts for the slow pace of his narrative. Reid falls somewhere in between. And as Defoe and Cooper captured the imagination of both young and old, so did Mayne Reid at the height of his fame. Although he can be firmly placed in the tradition of the juvenile adventure tale, his contributions to that tradition are unique.

II   *Reid's Rivals*

In order to place Reid in a contemporary context, it is necessary to understand the works of the four other major authors who wrote adventure stories for a voracious nineteenth-century reading public. Though these authors were immensely popular, their approaches were generally quite different.

Reid's immediate precursor was Frederick Marryat (1792 - 1848). Like Reid essentially a man of action, Marryat joined the British navy in 1806, and his naval experiences formed the basis for most of his fiction. He visited America in 1838, two years before Reid, but his only work with the United States as a setting was the nonfictional *Diary in America* (1839), which revealed his antidemocratic bias and distaste for everything American. Marryat wrote twenty-four novels; only the last four, written after his retirement from naval service, were written specifically for a juvenile audience. Unlike his earlier works, his juvenile titles are humorless, moralizing, and preaching. In keeping with the tradition of Defoe and Cooper, however, most of Marryat's adult sea stories were appropriated by his young readers, and it is upon them that his fame rests.

Marryat's best children's book, *Masterman Ready*, is important for comparison with Reid because of Marryat's interest in providing his readers with factual information. It was written to "improve" on *Swiss Family Robinson*, as Marryat was disturbed by the errors in geography and natural history prevalent in Wyss's book. Despite its Christian sermonizing, *Masterman Ready* makes absorbing reading even today. Marryat's realism in allowing the old seaman Ready to help the shipwrecked family survive on the island stands in contrast to the improbable encyclopedic knowledge of father Robinson in Wyss's book. In Marryat's story the education of the children is divided: Mr. Seagrave, the father, instructs his family in matters philosophical, while Ready provides advice on seamanship, agriculture, and carpentry.

Among Marryat's juvenile titles, only *Settlers in Canada* (1844) deals with the Western Hemisphere. In this improbable tale a family of landed aristocrats is forced to emigrate to Quebec. Once there, though the sons frolic in hunting expeditions, the family anxiously awaits a reversal of their fortunes so they can return to England. The book displays Marryat's cursory interest in Indians, but the vision is always eastward to the old country.

Like Marryat, William Henry Giles Kingston (1814 - 1880) wrote most of his stories about the sea. The geographical range of his works could be represented facetiously by one of his own titles, *Round the World: A Tale for Boys* (1859). And all around the world Kingston's purpose was to inspire his young readers with imperialistic ideals and Christian zeal. While America offered little opportunity of empire-building, there were still souls to be saved, and the heathen Red Indian was therefore a "natural" for Kingston. *In the Rocky Mountains* focuses on the conversion to Christianity of the Indian chiefs Winnemak and Piomingo; it preaches the lesson that conversion is the way to abolish Indian savagery, which is described by the author with relish. Although Kingston includes a great deal of exotic description of such phenomena as mud baths, sulfur springs, and geysers, the reader feels that both the natural settings and the adventures set therein function as a sugar-coating to the pill of learning lessons of virtue. "Is it not the duty of white men who are Christians," asks the author, "to send the blessed light of the gospel, by every means in their power, to their benighted fellow creatures?" (p. 315). Obviously, boys' books were the means in Kingston's power; his Indians are converted, become missionaries, and preach the gospel to their tribes. The same extraneous morality pervades *In the Wilds of Florida,* which has as its backdrop the Seminole War. Kingston tries to insert local color by introducing the problems of slavery and Indian affairs, but he is handicapped by his lack of familiarity with the subjects. Ignoring history, Kingston makes the Indian chief Osceola a dangerous, treacherous, and licentious man who lusts after the heroine and wants to force her into marriage.

By far the best of Reid's competitors was Robert Michael Ballantyne (1825 - 1894). Ballantyne, like Reid, had the advantage of extensive first-hand experience in North America. He had worked for several years as a trading-clerk with the Hudson's Bay Company, and used his knowledge to depict realistic scenes of wilderness life. Some fifteen of the seventy-one Ballantyne titles listed in the British Museum catalogue are set in North America, about half of them in Canada. The others run the gamut of sea stories, military tales, and animal stories, set in every part of the globe. Neither empire-building nor Christian moralizing is as obtrusive in Ballantyne's books as in the works of Marryat and Kingston, perhaps because the prevailing tone is so much lighter. Ballantyne is most famous for his South Sea "Robinsonnade," *The Coral Island,* which has added significance as the acknowledged model for William Golding's sophisticated twentieth-century "Robinsonnade," *Lord of the Flies.* In Ballantyne's book the first-person narrator is *not* the hero, thus giving it a natural, boyish quality not to be found in Marryat's shipwreck story. The three shipwrecked boys are quite human; they joke and clown, and do not always quest after knowledge.

Like most juvenile writers, Ballantyne is at his best when he concentrates on storytelling and lets the moral take care of itself, as in *The Dog Crusoe: A Tale of the Western Prairies* (1861), the book that many critics claim to be his best. This is a standard Western adventure tale with a twist—for there are two heroes: Dick Varley (a rather atypical frontier youth who saves the puppy, Crusoe, from an Indian stewpot) and the dog Crusoe himself. How can one fault a book which opens: "The dog Crusoe was once a pup"? Ballantyne demonstrates a delightful, dry wit as he delineates his dog-hero's history, speaking of him as a person whose litter-mates drowned "by falling into the river which flowed past the blockhouse—a calamity which occurred, doubtless, in consequence of their having gone out without their mother's leave" (p. 14). Anyone familiar with the usual nineteenth-century sermonizing at children finds this a welcome variation on the text of the dutiful child.

The last member of this quartet of storytellers, George Alfred Henty (1832 - 1902), shared honors with Kingston as a dedicated imperialist. Henty's work reflects this bias—although many of his books are historical in nature, the "modern" titles center around British interest in the new world. Henty was perhaps an armchair traveller, for in his preface to *In the Heart of the Rockies* he admits that he depends on United States government reports for details of the geography and scenery. In this book, Henty presents the standard English boy without prospects who goes to America to seek his fortune with his miner-uncle rather than take a job as a clerk in England. Henty's story line reveals the course that tradition had taken. Gone is the delight in exotic scenery; the emphasis is on a kind of Boy Scout adventure, rather tame despite the Indian attacks and the wild journey down the Colorado River rapids. The goal now is gold—not the buried treasure to be found by chance, but to be extracted by mining machinery requiring a large capital outlay. The tradition has degenerated (or perhaps gone full-circle back to Marryat), for here is a Horatio Alger/Horace Greeley story: the English youth goes West to make a fortune in order to return to England and live in the grand style. Adventure in America becomes the means to a success-oriented end rather than the end itself.

This brief survey of the major nineteenth-century adventure writers discloses three attitudes they held in common: first, a belief in the superiority of the white man (usually Anglo-Saxon); second, a tendency to preach, more or less insistently, the values of Christianity; third, a strong feeling of pride in the British Empire and its expansion. Even Ballantyne, the most restrained of the group, presents a world being developed by and for the British Empire.

III   *Reid's Innovations and Contributions*

In several ways Mayne Reid cannot be placed among such "typical" Victorian writers of adventure tales. According to Henry Steele Commager's comparison of English and American children's literature, Reid is in some ways far more "American" than British:

English children's literature displays the sense of advent; the feeling for Empire . . . the deep feeling for nature tamed and neat. . . . From American literature emerges a different picture; equalitarianism . . . adventure, but of a different kind—adventure in the American west rather than in distant lands, adventure that makes not for imperialism but as often as not for provincialism; courage, hatred of the bully; self-reliance; work and the gospel of work; nature in the raw rather than tamed . . . humor that ran to the boisterous and the tall story rather than to whimsy or non-sense.[5]

While Reid's stance incorporates both of Commager's categories, he is certainly more the "American." He is so equalitarian at times that he substitutes political sermonizing for the religious sermonizing of his contemporaries. He is famous for his use of American western settings, and nearly all of his work contains the American brand of humor mentioned by Commager. To this may be added Reid's extreme fidelity to scientific accuracy and his unusual racial tolerance, both of which distinguish him from his contemporaries.

Children are known to respond positively to facts, and Reid offered them a kind of reality even in his most improbable plots. His children's books present a scientifically correct natural world. But his adventure tales are more than scientifically accurate; they are true to the *spirit* of real adventure. Geoffrey Trease tells us that "the real adventurer is impelled by many motives: geographical curiosity, a passion for archaeology or anthropology, or botany or some other science, humanitarianism or political ideals. The fictional hero is allowed none of these, least of all the last" (p. 108). In most of his juvenile work Reid cannot be faulted here, for these very motives that Trease finds so rare most frequently inspire Reid's characters—unlike those of Kingston and Henty.

Reid's juvenile titles fall into three categories: "Robinsonnades," "hunt-and-chase" tales (thinly disguised dissertations on geography and natural history), and "dime novels." All, in one way or another, contain the "useful knowledge" so admired by the Victorians. Of the group, the hunting books are the most didactic and the dime novels the least. Reid's first children's book, *The Desert Home* (1852), is also his best—no doubt because of its close adherence to the "Robinsonnade" formula.

IV   Reid's "Robinsonnade"

The America of *The Desert Home* (1852) held a number of charms for British youth. Reid shows that a "Robinsonnade" need not have an island setting, for here the party of travellers finds its haven in a valley oasis in the midst of the Great American Desert (somewhere on the eastern slope of the Staked Plains), painstakingly described in the opening chapters. The novel's relevance to British readers is apparent, for the Rolfe family are in fact English emigrés; the father, having dissipated his fortune in the old world, believes he can recover it in the United States. But there are problems in America too. Robert Rolfe's first attempt to win wealth by buying a Virginia plantation is doomed to failure because of the evils of the slavery system, as he confesses: "There were no laborers to be had in the place—except such as were slaves. . . . Purchasing a number of blacks, both men and women, I began life as a planter. After such a bargain as that, I did not deserve to prosper; and I did not prosper" (p. 45). It should be noted that Reid indicts slavery and the slave trade in every juvenile title where his characters encounter it. This is particularly evident in his sea stories. For example, in *Ran Away to Sea* (1858), Reid makes his stowaway's vessel a slaver in order to attack the system and its horrors, which he describes in great detail.

The failure of the plantation impels the family on its westward trek. Reid makes it clear that America, the land of opportunity for his English family, can be found only through a retreat from civilization; his narrator observes, "the harsh treatment we had received at the hands of civilized man—buffeted about by ill-fortune—continually deceived, and at every step becoming poorer and more dependent, all had their effect in blunting that desire I should otherwise have felt to get back to the world" (p. 134).

The Rolfe family carries with it the Protestant ethic, though the bountiful and beautiful valley inspires religious sentiments of a different kind as well. Indeed, that most Protestant of creatures, the beaver, provides the basis for the family's industry. Good empirical Englishmen, they observe that the beautiful lake formed in the valley has been caused by a beaver dam, and that the pelts of the beavers will provide the material prosperity they seek. Thus the discovery of a land where wealth can be drawn from nature and need not depend on the vagaries of men is a cause for rejoicing. All the while the family is busy storing up this fur-gold, it is also enriching itself spiritually in the beauty and serenity of the valley. Here man is clearly in control (even the children are able to tame wild animals for pets), yet nature exists in a wild and free state about them. The value of the experience may be inferred from the fact that the family spends ten years in the valley; they leave only in order to educate the children properly, and then return to their oasis to settle permanently—strong testimony indeed to the material and spiritual value of this escape from civilization.

Of course there is an element of fairytale in all this. The America of *The Desert Home* is also a land of hostile Indians, who kill mothers and children swiftly and without tears. These ogre Indians are just as unrealistic as the extravagantly successful Rolfe family. The *Athenaeum* reviewer noted the improbability of "discovering and turning to account the rich and various productions of Nature to live in greater luxury and comfort than the most sophisticated gentry," and doubted that "any children who have got beyond the age of believing in the faery beanstalk, take romances like Captain Mayne Reid's for gospel" (February 14, 1852, p. 198).

It is quite likely, however, that children who had accepted other "Robinsonnades" equally marvelous and less specifically located would accept *The Desert Home's* marvels as fact. And Reid was to adapt the "Robinsonnade" formula frequently in his children's books, changing the setting but repeating many of the same adventures. For example, *The Forest Exiles* (1854), *The Bush Boys* (1855), and *Afloat in the Forest* (1866) all have families existing off the land and trying to make their fortunes in exotic wilderness settings from South America to South Africa. Significantly, however, only in *The Desert Home* (the only "Robinsonnade" set in America) do the characters return to settle permanently at the site of their adventures. Once again we see the power of the biographical fantasy, this time influencing Reid in a direction diametrically opposed to that of his contemporaries.

V *The Hunt-and-Chase Tale: or, Journeys Through Fields of Science and Adventure*

Reid's second type of juvenile fiction, the "hunt-and-chase" story, is a variation on the travelogue storybook that was to become so popular in the nineteenth century. The period's fashion for semifictional travel adventures undoubtedly began with Samuel Griswold Goodrich's *Tales of Peter Parley about America* (1827) and its sequels and imitations. Goodrich firmly believed that children needed truth rather than fiction; he wanted to replace such fictional creations of the imagination as monsters, giants, and fairies with history, natural history, geography, and biography. Hence the moral and educational tone of all his works.

Reid must have been aware of the success of Goodrich's travel books as well as of the tremendous interest in natural history in an era marked by the explosion of scientific knowledge. Reid was among the first to combine the three elements of educational travel, exciting adventures, and zoological information into the fictional form represented by these "hunt-and-chase" tales. Although by the 1880's many juvenile authors were fabricating adventure tales by sending parties of young people off on strange travel paths, Mayne Reid did this as early as 1853 with *The Boy Hunters*, followed that same year with a sequel, *The Young Voyageurs*, which takes place in Canada. In 1855, with *The Hunter's Feast*, Reid returned to writing adult fiction by adapting his successful juvenile formula, with adults instead of children as principal characters. But he continued writing these books throughout his career. The settings of most works are apparent from their titles.

The plot of *The Boy Hunters* is a simple one. Colonel Landi, formerly of Napoleon's army, has retired to Louisiana with his three young sons and a faithful manservant. In his retirement the colonel enjoys the best of all possible worlds as a hunter-naturalist. A letter arrives from Charles Lucien, Napoleon's naturalist brother, who has his heart set on obtaining the skin of a white buffalo. As their father is too old for the arduous task, the boys set out on the hunt, accompanied by the faithful manservant. This of course is a ploy to get the characters out of doors where Reid can describe nature. Some of the education his boy-readers had to swallow along with the adventures was very forced: "'Would it not be interesting, Basil,' said François, appealing to his older brother, 'if Lucien would give us a botanical description of all these trees and tell us their uses'" (p. 84). Lucian promptly responds with a disquisition on the mulberry, that most utilitarian of trees. In this manner a great deal of "useful information" is imparted, assuming that the boy-reader did not skip such passages to get on to the next exciting chase.

Today we would condemn this as pedantry, or at best as an attempt to insert "useful knowledge" into children's books, which should be spontaneous and imaginative. We might object to Reid as a children's author masquerading as a moralist and scholar. However, bright children seeking knowledge would devour Reid's work eagerly and all mid-nineteenth-century children undoubtedly were less offended by Reid's lessons in natural history than they were by those authors who lectured to them endlessly about personal cleanliness and religious behavior.

One important feature of *The Boy Hunters* and Reid's other books of its kind is their threefold philosophical purpose which conveniently encompasses Reid's own primary interests: scientific, political, and social. In *The Boy Hunters* Reid uses nature to explain scientific theory in Chapter XI, "The Chain of Destruction," which depicts the survival of the fittest in a little drama witnessed by the boys. A tarantula kills a hummingbird and is in turn devoured by a chameleon, which is then attacked by a scorpion lizard. The lizard is swallowed by a snake, who is conquered by a kite. The kite falls prey to an eagle, which is then shot by Basil, "the last link." Here America functions merely as a backdrop for the dramatic enactment of nature's struggle for existence: a backdrop more appropriate and exotic than that of the English countryside.

Reid's second use of nature is political. In contrast to most other writers of juvenile fiction who were arch-conservatives, Reid introduced radically republican views into his work. How much this influenced his audience is difficult to say, but his hunt-and-chase tales are full of comments such as:

He derives his name of "king vulture" not from the possession of any noble qualities, but from the manner in which he tyrannizes over the *common* vultures, (*aura* and *atratus*), keeping them from their food until he has gorged himself with the choicest morsels. In this sense the name is most appropriate; as such conduct presents a striking analogy to that of most human kinds toward the *common* people. (p. 327)

Reid also uses nature to make philosophic statements on racial issues. He tries to treat Indians fairly both in the abstract and the concrete. An example of the former is Lucien's story about the turkey buzzards—a "what's mine is mine and what's yours is mine" tale that is "intended to illustrate the superior cunning of the white over the Indian race, and is a pretty fair example of the honesty and justice which the former has too often observed in its dealings with the latter" (p. 302). Reid's desire to be fair is worked out concretely on the plot level when the boys are saved from death at the hands of the Indians because the mysterious pipe Colonel Landi gave Basil to wear around his neck in an embroidered pouch turns out to be the calumet of Tecumseh's brother, "The Prophet." Swayed by their belief in the talisman's power, the Indians help the boys find their white buffalo and then escort them safely home. This humanization and individual treatment of the Red Indian differentiates Reid from many of his peers. His Indians can be good men without having been converted to Christianity; they are, in part at least, people instead of objects. And this same humanitarian spirit characterizes Reid's treatment of native peoples wherever they are to be found in his juvenile travellers' world.

VI   *Dealings with the House of Beadle and Adams*

Reid wrote a third type of juvenile fiction: the "dime novel." This type is intermediary between the strictly juvenile works discussed above and the adult romances, some of which were reissued in dime-novel form in later years, both in America and England. The dime novel in America (which roughly corresponds to the English penny-dreadful of the same period) reached its height in the publications of the firm of Beadle and Adams.[6] Beadle and Adams novels were often published in England in the same format as in America, merely substituting an illustration of a sixpence for that of the dime on the cover. Reid wrote five original stories for dime-novel publication; all were written after his health had deteriorated and his finances declined, when he depended heavily on revenue from Beadle and Adams to support himself.[7] The poor quality of the "original" dime novels is evident in *The White Squaw* which, bound with *The Yellow Chief*, is the only Beadle and Adams title held by the British Museum.

The White Squaw, first published by Beadle and Adams in 1869, takes place in Florida, a locale Reid had already used to advantage in *Oçeola*, but this work is more in the tradition of the English penny-dreadful, whose short sentences and paragraphs and lack of descriptive detail result from writers' being paid a penny-a-line. Several factual errors uncharacteristic of Reid appear in this tale. The Seminole Indians are inaccurately described as living in wigwams, so that we cannot in this instance praise his fidelity to Indian customs. His chronology is equally skewed, for the time is set about 1860, long after the Seminole War which is supposed to be in progress. In *The White Squaw* Reid is slipshod in his plotting and characterization: the story opens with Warren Rody, son of the evil "governor" of the Tampa Bay settlement, saving the life of Nelatu, son of the Seminole chief, Oluski. This heroic deed, plus the description of Warren clad in buckskin, leads the reader to believe he has been introduced to a standard hero. Such expectations are exploded on Warren's second appearance, however, when he is described as being small, effeminate, and foppishly dressed. And indeed he turns out to be a subsidiary villain who seduces Sansuta, Nelatu's sister, causing Oluski to fall in a fit and die. Warren's own sister, Alice, is a pure, angelic heroine who enchants all, including the stock Natty Bumppo backswoodman Cris Carrol and the real hero, Wacora, Oluski's nephew and chief of a neighboring tribe, a man who dreams of uniting all the tribes into one nation. After Nelatu discovers his sister's love nest, he kills Warren, causing Sansuta to go mad and play Ophelia, comforted by Alice who has become a captive of the Indians and a great favorite with them. Wacora (whose mother, also an Indian captive, was a white woman) marries Alice, who thereby becomes the white squaw of the title. Alice's conversion from Indian-hater to Indian's bride, required by the exigencies of the plot, is not supported by adequate character delineation. At the beginning of the story when Nelatu admires Alice she tartly tells her brother Warren, "I am a white woman—he is an Indian. How dare you speak of such a thing?" (p. 52); when at the conclusion she thinks of Wacora as "one of Nature's noblemen" (p. 119) the reader is unconvinced.

Reid also depicts a double-died villain right out of the gothic tale in the Negro Crookleg, who resembles Chakra from *The Maroon*. And yet Reid builds sympathy for Crookleg by showing his villainy as having its roots in slavery and giving us glimpses of the man beneath the mask: "My mother was a slave, but she war my mother for all dat, an' if I war a black man I was still a human bein', although you and de likes of you didn't think so" (p. 94). This indictment of slavery in the Crookleg character, the choice of an Indian as the hero of the story, and the potential for racial amalgamation in the love of Alice and Wacora again indicate Reid's variations from the stereotypes of other British authors.

The Yellow Chief (1869) is a more representative work in that Reid here follows his frequent custom of using explanatory footnotes about events and nomenclature unfamiliar to an English audience. The story opens on the Mississippi plantation of Squire

Blackadder as his son commands the overseer to punish the mulatto
Blue Dick by dousing him under the water pump. This "old and oft
repeated tableau of master and slave" (p. 6) is used to establish the
evils of slavery and to give Blue Dick a motive for running away.
That no good can come of slavery is seen in the next chapter, set
five years later. The squire, bankrupt, emigrates to the West in a
caravan with his lovely daughter Clara and his remaining slaves.
They are ambushed and captured by Cheyennes led by the
mysterious "yellow" (i.e., mulatto) chief, Blue Dick. Ned O'Neil
and Elijah Orton (Reid's standard British adventurer and his standard trapper companion) observe the attack and go to St. Vrain's
Fort for assistance from the trappers, who are led by "Black
Harris." Meanwhile, Blue Dick is subjecting his old enemies to the
water torture, including Clara, notwithstanding the fact that she has
been revealed to be his half-sister. The trappers come to the rescue
and Clara is reunited with Ned, her old lover whom her father had
rejected in his more prosperous days. Ned sells his Tipperary estates
and invests in Manhattan real estate where he and his bride live
happily ever after.

This too is a patently absurd story, although more straightforward
than *The White Squaw*. The antislavery theme remains, and the
narrative gets some interest from the graphic descriptions of real
places like St. Vrain's Fort and real people like Moses Harris.[8] And
once more the hero chooses to remain in the United States. Despite
the absurdity of its plot, *The Yellow Chief* is elevated by the imaginative appeal of Reid's descriptions. He has a sincere admiration
for the rough mountain men whom he depicts realistically and does
not attempt to idealize. And Reid's enthusiasm for the Far West of
his setting permeates his description of the countryside and reminds
us of his own dream: "Were I to live in the not very remote future, I
would rather have in my ornamental grounds the ruins of one of
Bent's or St. Vrain's Forts, than the crumbling walls of Kenilworth
Castle or the Keep of Carisbrooke. More picturesquely romantic,
more exalting, would be the souvenirs recalled, and the memories
awakened by them" (p. 60).

Aside from these considerations, *The Yellow Chief* is escapism
pure and simple, and answers very well Frederick Whittaker's
description of the dime novel in general:

If my recollection serves me rightly, vice was always vanquished and virtue
always triumphant in the dime novel. . . . The tendency of this class of
literature is to fill a boy's mind with a certain longing to get away from the

old home, as soon as he is big enough to shoulder a rifle, and to take part in the scenes which he has read of with such feverish impatience. . . . These stories undoubtedly do give a boy a false view of life, make him dissatisfied in certain respects with the every-day world around him, and fill his mind with dreams of deeds and heroism in which he is to be the chief actor.[9]

There is abundant evidence that many British boys were lured to America in fact as well as fancy by such tales. One testimonial to this effect comes from Godfrey Sykes, who spent his boywood in a quiet English country village. In his autobiography, *A Westerly Trend* (Tucson, 1944), he tells how he felt a " 'call of the wild' and an urge for the open places. The tangential impulse came at length, and quite unmistakably, from the pages of a somewhat lurid tale of adventure upon the plains of Texas. Captain Mayne Reid . . . was the author" (p. 17). So off Sykes went. In his case the result was beneficial; he established a professional reputation as geologist and engineer in the West that had first thrilled him in Reid's pages.

The War Trail (London, 1857) is a different kind of dime novel. It was first published as an "adult" romance and was not issued in dime-novel format until 1882. The plot of *The War Trail* (discussed in greater detail in the previous chapter) is so convoluted that Reid himself is unable to untangle its various skeins. Briefly recapitulated, a band of Texas Rangers led by Captain Edward Warfield is sent to guard a Mexican village from hostile Comanches. Warfield falls in love with Doña Isolina, whose father, Don Ramon Vargas, is "Ayankiedo" (i.e., friendly to Americans). Doña Isolina expresses a desire for a certain wild horse, which gives Warfield a chance to chase it and while so doing to battle and describe nature and its creatures. The Comanche, "the *fiend* of the Texan settler" (p. 141), is yet less despicable than the cowardly Mexican represented by the villain Ijurras, who had been a spy during the late Texas war. Ijurras is after Isolina and tries to blackmail her into marriage; but is foiled by Warfield, who defeats him in a duel. Ijurras then plans to ambush Warfield in the forest, but the hero is saved by his friend the naturalist Elijah Quackenboss, who is conveniently on the spot—plant-hunting. After the Rangers leave the village, the guerillas return to multilate the women who had fraternized with the Americans. Isolina escapes this horrid fate on horseback, but when her steed runs wild the rangers must chase her, aided by trapper Rube Rawlings. She is captured by Indians but craftily rescued by Warfield, disguised as a chief's son, and the lovers are reunited.

In the original version of this complex story, Reid had inter-

polated long passages of nature description and philosophical dis-
quisitions on politics and racial relations. Many of these were
deleted from the dime-novel version. The changes are interesting.
Reid omits the whole of the first descriptive apostrophe chapter and
jumps right into the narrative. There are no comments on
despotism, no autobiographical asides, less self-pity and introspection. There is a rapid acceleration and telescoping of the events of
chase and rescue, more dialogue and action, less love. In a way this
is an improvement; Reid is content to describe the beauties of land
and lady once only.

As the Beadle and Adams edition of *The War Trail* was published
in 1882, twenty-five years after the original, it is possible that some
deletions were made for a new generation of young readers to
whom the issues of Mexican treachery and Texan bravery were no
longer relevant. However, they more probably were made to con-
serve space and to quicken the pace and thus be more suitable for a
juvenile audience.

The dime novel, whether written directly for such publication or
adapted for it from a larger work, is a transitional type between
juvenile and adult fiction. It combines features of the adventure tale
with those of sensational and sentimental fiction, so that aspects of
gothic terror or pride in Anglo-Saxon superiority can frequently be
found in the exotic setting of America. The dime novel, as Merle
Curti has pointed out, was the nearest thing to a proletarian
literature "written for the great masses of people and actually read
by them."[10] It was appropriate that Reid, so radical in his political
beliefs, should have produced so many of them. Today they are
merely historical curiosities, but in their time, with the spread of
popular education, new readers liked works that made individual effort seem important. Dime novels stressed self-reliance and achievement, and their attempt to promote a spirit of adventure and rugged individualism resulted in the apotheosis of the frontiersman
hero who conquered evils by personal rather than group or social
action. The dime novel also, in Curti's words, "exalted the
American people above all others. . . . In emphasizing the uni-
queness and the superiority of American scenery, institutions, and
especially, American character, the dime novel must have enhanced
national pride and patriotic devotion in the minds of the masses of
readers" (p. 769). Such pictures of America no doubt made a powerful impression on the English audience and stimulated great interest in America.

The boys who read Mayne Reid absorbed a picture of America—its landscape, people, and institutions—which was very different from the America presented in the works of his fellow British authors. That picture developed in part from Reid's personality, shaped as it was by the memory of his experiences in America. Very much an individualist, Reid transmitted his love of freedom and hatred of slavery to a young English audience in need of such ideas so different from those expressed by many of their other favorite authors. Reid's appreciation of the beauties of wild nature, his practical scientific knowledge, and his conception of the intrinsic worth of each human being regardless of color set him apart from the more mundane authors who also wrote juvenile fiction.

The fame of Mayne Reid as a juvenile author does not rest exclusively on those works directed specifically to his boy-readers, but upon his adult romances as well, which his admirers eventually claimed for themselves. As they had done with Defoe and Cooper, the children had taken Reid for their own.

CHAPTER 4

Reid's Victorian Appeal

I The Reading Public

ONE of Mayne Reid's novels was translated into Russian under the title *A Dream Come True*, a title symbolic of Reid's appeal to a worldwide audience. Although sales figures are hard to ascertain, especially in view of the many pirated versions of Reid's work, Altick's survey of "railway novels" (yellowbacks in library series) includes Reid in these "veritable rosters of Victorian bestsellerdom" (p. 299). Perhaps the circulating libraries of the time are a better indication of Reid's popularity. Mudie's was among the most famous of these libraries, and Sara Keith's tabulation of Mudie's holdings for the years 1848 - 69 validates Reid's firm position with the reading public. Mudie stocked twenty Reid titles, which compares favorably with such other authors as Cooper (41), Scott (32), Marryat (24), Dickens (23), Thackeray (15), and Ballantyne (11). These figures are especially significant since Reid's first novel was not published until 1850.[1] Mudie's 1928 *Catalogue* lists thirty-five Reid titles, an indication of his continuing popularity with this audience. Another indication of Reid's ability to transcend space and time is his popularity with foreign readers in mid-twentieth century. *The Index Translationum* (Paris: UNESCO, 1958 - 58) shows that translations of Reid's works were published in Belgium, Brazil, Bulgaria, Czechoslovakia, Denmark, Finland, France, Germany, Hungary, Iran, Israel, Italy, Mexico, The Netherlands, Poland, Portugal, Rumania, Spain, the U.S.S.R., and Yugoslavia. The most popular book has been *The Headless Horseman*, closely followed by *Rifle Rangers, Scalp Hunters, White Chief, Oçeola*, and *The Quadroon*. Reid has been especially popular with Eastern European readers from the mid-nineteenth century to the present; *Headless Horseman* was reprinted in Russia in 1967.

Back in the "prosperous fifties" of the Victorian Age when Reid began to write, he drew upon an enlarged reading public whose leisure time was largely devoted to "light reading": literature that made minimal demands upon its audience. However, the belief was widespread that the new class of readers would constantly improve their taste in books. Thus the writing of popular literature could be defended as a means of reaching the minds of those unable to respond at once to "true" literature. As most studies of the period show, reading taste moved steadily toward entertainment, both in fiction and nonfiction. The great popularity of periodicals like *Cassell's Illustrated Family Paper* contributed to the change in reading tastes and the broadening of the reading public, especially after the abolition of the paper duty in 1861. Directed at a family audience, such journals began to stress adventure fiction more than sentimental romance. Eventually, however, the two genres came together to present the blend of romance with sensational themes so well represented by Reid's *The Maroon*, published in *Cassell's* from January 18 - July 19, 1862. The sensational emphasis is apparent in the illustrations to the text; they depict its violent and even implicitly sexual scenes in the best gothic tradition—a strange choice of emphasis for a "family paper." It may be that the inferior quality of Reid's later novels, with their short chapters and sensational suspense at the end of each installment derives from such serial publication, which had an important effect on the development of English popular fiction.[2]

These romantic and sensational elements seldom stood alone in Victorian fiction. Reid chose to superimpose them on the solid factual foundation of the Defoe tradition and thus to appeal to readers who wanted to learn about people and places very different from those they knew. And just as Crusoe's adventures derived their appeal to an eighteenth-century British audience from the economic individualism that could be practiced in a simple agrarian isolation, so Reid's largely autobiographical heroes appealed to an increasingly urban, industrialized, and puritanic Victorian Britain.

Reid's romances offered "respectable" satisfaction (as opposed to the great body of pornography in the period) to a public anxious for the ideal and the exotic as release from the anxiety of an increasingly complex world. This was a public which gloried in the Crystal Palace and preferred not to think of the working conditions in the glass factories which produced the huge glass bubble that so astonished them. Reid did not hold these readers without being aware of their taste in the sensational, the sentimental, the exotic, the scientific, and the melodramatic. His fiction shows how well he understood it. Readers who sought escape in fiction liked stories to which they could transfer their own conflicts metaphorically; the form of melodramatic romance, while seeming to promote the idea that virtue was its own reward, in reality proved that virtue had very material rewards to offer. This idea was pervasive in the popular culture of the period, as is evident not only in the penny press but also in the theaters, where melodrama was the prevailing form.[3] Reid's novels, of course, contain both sensationalism and sentimentality (mixed with scientific data about distant lands) and thus have an even wider appeal.

II   The Lure of Distant Lands

The travel tale was an ideal form for an audience that wanted knowledge as well as escape. It had been common practice for eighteenth-century novelists to adapt travel accounts to fictional form, but those who continued this practice in the nineteenth century were catering to a new class of readers whose passionate interest in foreign lands came from their conception of empire: these were lands to be fought for, to be explored, and to serve as outlets for English emigration. The nineteenth-century passion for travel tales is apparent from contemporary reviews as well as from the research of twentieth-century scholars.[4] The two primary reasons for the popularity of such works were the burgeoning interest in science and the subject of emigration. Both are apparent in a *British Quarterly Review* article on five books about the Western Hemisphere which stresses the value of their verisimilitude and comments: "Have the sons of our noble families, or of our rich merchants, a year or two to spare after their book education is completed, and before they enter on the struggles of actual life—they set off to India, to California, to the Cape. . . . The pressure of population in England sends forth many travellers" (May 1852, p. 339). The article indicates that books set in America presenting scientific information in an interesting form would have widespread appeal. And indeed this kind of genre appeared in large numbers, often in the form of the hunting travel book.

In the nineteenth century, America was one of the favorite haunts of British sportsmen, many of whom published factual hunting narratives. In a scientific age, the naturalist was held in high esteem, and most of the hunters took pains to assume this posture. In 1879 John Mortimer Murphy published in London *Sporting Adventures in the Far West,* an account of seven years spent in western

America. His book consists of eighteen chapters, each devoted to a different kind of American animal, from the favorite grizzly bear, buffalo, moose, and deer, through the Rocky-Mountain goat and raccoon. The book is essentially a mélange of his adventures with comments on strange people and places and advice on the procedures of the hunt. Murphy tries to transcribe American dialects accurately and gives rather full accounts of American customs, cautioning his English readers on the need to behave democratically in a democratic land. Of primary interest, however, is Murphy's conception of himself as a scientist. In his "Preface" he notes, "I devoted particular attention to studying the fauna of the country, especially the game, whether it was fur, fin, or feather. . . . Some of my hunting was as much for the purpose of studying the *ferae naturae* as for killing them." Murphy here follows Reid, who established the scientific travelogue in his fiction more than two decades earlier. Indeed, Reid's devotion to science often damages the progress of his plot. For example, in *The Quadroon* he stresses the need for verisimilitude of setting and then goes on to describe the Louisiana flora and fauna, "the 'catalpa,' with its silvery bark and trumpet-shaped blossoms; the 'Osage orange,' with its dark shining leaves . . . the cactacaae of varied forms. . . . The mock-bird pipes from the top of the tallest magnolia; his cousin, the red-breast half intoxicated with the berries of the melia, rivals him in his sweet song" (pp. 99, 100 - 01). Reid combined fiction and natural history to satisfy the twin manias of the public. And his scientific accuracy was respected in his own time. On October 27, 1883, the *Spectator* even went so far as to say of Reid "in our judgment he missed his true career, and would have made a first-class agent of the Geographical Society" (p. 1374). Thus to his romances, highly colored with melodrama and depicting places and persons of great interest to British readers, Reid added yet another ingredient: the scientific veracity that was recognized as part of his audience appeal.

Part of the "dream come true" for Victorian England was the tangible benefit to be derived from increased scientific knowledge. Knowledge came to be accepted as the first step to power, and for many a uniquely symbolic power inhered in the ability to name and thereby to know the elements of plant and animal life. Thus Reid's practice of persistently naming all the species of nature served a real interest and need for his contemporaries. Yet in spite of this "scientific" stance, Mayne Reid is essentially a carryover from the Romantic Age. For him, like the earlier Romantics, nature was a symbol of freedom; he never accepted the later conception of nature as a symbol of law.

The search for entertaining knowledge on the part of the English reading public was not confined to the realm of science. Another topic captured their attention early in the century: "tourist" travel tales. The interest of the British in their transatlantic cousins was well served by British authors—to their own and their publisher's profit. This was recognized by such an authority as Tony Weller of *Pickwick Papers*, whose advice apropos Pickwick's escape from Fleet Street Prison and threatened bankruptcy was that he "have a passage ready taken for 'Merriker. . . . Let him come back and write a book about the 'Merrikins as'll pay all his expenses and more, if he blows 'em up enough."

Many reasons have been suggested for British interest in America, from the blatantly financial one implied in Mr. Weller's quip to more complex promptings of familial ties or racial kinship between the two countries. Englishmen wrote travel books by the score, but when it came to transmitting the glamour of travel in the guise of fiction, British authors were more hesitant. Myron Brightfield's reading of two thousand novels published in England from 1840 - 60 led him to the conclusion that fictional accounts of America were severely limited by their authors' unfamiliarity with the subject. Victorian novelists who sought to depict manners realistically would naturally hesitate before attempting the unknown. According to Brightfield, "to compose caricatures of Americans for purposes of farce might indeed require little knowledge of them or their country; but for the dedicated realist no true portrayal could emerge from less than an extended acquaintance with, and observation of, the subject matter. In the absence of such familiarity, the attempt was to be declined. Thackeray believed that no one could write creditably on the United States without five years' residence there. Anthony Trollope declared plaintively that the powers of the realist were often overtaxed even by the requirements of depicting English life."[5] Unlike so many of his countrymen, Mayne Reid certainly qualified as a resident-expert on the basis of his twelve years' intermittent residence in America. Despite the melodramatic and gothic quality of his novels, there was enough verisimilitude in them derived from that actual experience and observation to make them convincing to both English and American audiences.[6] Readers appreciated the qualities of realism in even the wildest of his romances, as most contemporary reviews indicate.

Many of his readers who planned to emigrate would require verisimilitude from Reid. The reports of American emigrés were widely published and Wilbur S. Shepperson's comment about these books could be used as a description of Mayne Reid's American works—those which became significant "did so because of the sheer force of the author's personality. Such works were designed as emotional and subjective revelation. . . . For three centuries the Americas had been a land of quests, and nineteenth-century romanticism found its new institutions, new freedoms, and new society irresistible."[7] Certainly the characters and situations of Reid's novels are lifted from a pedestrian level primarily because of the author's enthusiasm for his American setting.

As is evident both from Reid's biography and from the idealistic view of America developed in his novels, Mayne Reid himself viewed this country as a land of quests. His conception resembles the definition given by Charles L. Sanford in *The Quest for Paradise* (Urbana: University of Illinois Press, 1961): "Most images of paradise would seem in some sense to express an assertion of individual or group freedom and self government as against the constaints of parental or societal authority." Sanford believes that the underlying assumption is that human beings "act to better their lives. . . . The freedom that is desired is the fancied freedom to be enjoyed in a luxuriant state of nature, as opposed to the censorship, the rules and regulations, the economic deprivations, the class distinctions, the forms and ceremonies . . . the tyranny of rules, the burden of taxes, the responsibilities of adulthood, the boredom of routine—the very complexities of social relationships experienced in advanced stages of ancient or modern civilization" (pp. 12 - 15). These themes recur frequently in Reid's work as the romantic dream that shaped his career. As he states in *Hunter's Feast:* "Lost on the prairie you are alone; but you are free" (p. 25).

Reid thus helped to perpetuate the myth of America as the earthly paradise. Other British visitors were aware of the changing face of mid-century America. As Marvin Fisher points out in his excellent study, *Workshops in the Wilderness* (New York: Oxford Univ. Press, 1967), these visitors registered both surprise and admiration as responses to the new American technology, for they had "expected to find an agricultural nation where men with a few hand tools worked in harmony with Nature; instead they found a land where, as many variously phrased it, 'manufactories simply spring out of the ground,' and where 'steam was the national element' by which men 'annihilated space and time' " (p. 47). Reid preferred to transcend space and time via the medium of romance for, considering the time he spent in industrial areas like Pennsylvania and New York, he surely must have been aware of the growing industrialization of this country. Reid's view was retrospective and romantic like that of some European visitors who, according to Fisher, held fast to the agrarian myth, for the "American landscape, fertile prairie and old forest, still fitted the dream-conception of the European romantic" (p. 37). Reid appeals to this dream-conception, especially in the later works, when he himself was far removed in time and space from the land he loved. The following representative passage from *Death Shot* (1873) suggests the appeal of this promise of freedom and potential: "In the midst of this verdant expanse, less than a quarter of a century ago, man was rarely met. . . . Since then he has entered upon, and scratched a portion of its surface; though not much, compared with its immensity. There are still grand expanses of the Texan prairie unfurrowed by the plowshare of the colonist—almost untrodden by the foot of the explorer. Even at this hour, the traveller may journey for days on grass-grown plains, amidst groves of timber, without seeing . . . so much as a chimney rising above the tree-tops" (p. 168). Reid interpreted his data in such a manner that what emerges on his pages is an America seen through a glass, brightly. To modern readers who have read their history books, it is obvious that Reid's America never existed on this earth, but only in the backward glance of a romantic expatriate—and in the eager and responsive imaginations of his armchair British readers.

Perhaps Reid was a captive of his own self-image—one strongly reminiscent of that described by R. W. B. Lewis as "the image of a radically new personality, the hero of the new adventure: an individual emancipated from history, happily bereft of ancestry, untouched and undefiled by the usual inheritances of family and race; an individual standing alone, self-reliant and self-propelling, ready to confront whatever awaited him."[8] Lewis's description applied to Reid reinforces his curiously Anglo-American split. While Reid resembles other English authors who emphasize the physical dangers of exotic lands, his works lack several characteristics of the type—invariable native villainy, the passion for gold, the return to England, etc., which do not appear because they represent cultural values which Reid has rejected. As a zealous "convert" to Americanism, Reid in his denouements denies rather than affirms the values of English society, and his "Westerns"—close spiritual descendants of *Walden*—are more about how to get away than how to get ahead. The heroes of his tales would say with Thoreau, "Eastward I go by force, but Westward I go free." They do not exploit the land and then leave it. Rather they become one with the land, turning it to good use for both material profit and spiritual solace.

III *Mayne Reid's Women*

Reid shares Anglo-American Victorian sentiments about love and the perfection of the family circle (his postmarital epilogues always depict a sacrosanct hearth with beaming parents and blissful babes). However, perhaps because of the blood and thunder of his tales, Reid's attitude toward romantic love varies slightly from the norms of Victorian society. His heroines, particularly those of Mexican ancestry, behave in love relationships with altogether more freedom than their English counterparts. A display of passion is allowed them, and a modern reader discerns symbolic hints in such recurring actions as the heroine's mount running off with a band of wild mustangs and the hero in hot pursuit, replete with allusions to taming both woman and mare. Such scenes are rudely Lawrencean, and D. H. Lawrence may have been aware of this himself on the evidence of the reading taste of Henry Grenfel, the hero of "The Fox," who often "walked about the fields and along the edges alone in the dark at night, prowling with a queer instinct for the night, and listening to the wild sounds. Tonight, however, he took a Captain Mayne Reid book from Banford's shelf and sat down with his knees wide apart and immersed himself in his story."[9] The violent chase of woman by man, symbolically evident in much of Lawrence, is set by Reid invariably in America, perhaps suggesting that America is the land where the emotions too can have greater freedom. This is reinforced by scenes such as that in *Headless Horseman* when the American heroine visits the hero's hut and becomes disturbed when he does *not* make advances. This undercurrent of the passionate woman and the renegade in Reid's work is certainly atypical of Victorian codes of "respectability." While all these women are not set in the Western Hemisphere, their prototypes are, for Reid's heroines, like his heroes, do not deviate from the standard established in his early works—all of which depict America and its people. As usual, Reid does this both because it is what he does best and because it is what his readers are most interested in.

Reid follows Cooper in using paired heroines, brunette and

blonde, masculine and feminine, active and passive. But he breaks
with tradition in that he sometimes allows his dark heroines (even
when their darkness comes from mixed blood) to win their way to
marital bliss. A good example is Marian Holt, the dark sister and
Diana character of *Wild Huntress,* who has a "heart endowed with
courage equal to that of a man." Reid gives her plenty of opportunity to display that courage as she lives with the Indians in order to
escape a forced marriage, leads the charge to rescue her sister
Lillian from the vile Mormons, and otherwise performs heroic
deeds. And Reid is more successful than Cooper in depicting such
American women believably. Any woman who could and would
participate in such adventures would probably have considerably
more success than Cooper grants such a character as Cora Munroe
of *The Last of the Mohicans* (1826). Reid allows Frank Wingrove to
marry Marian, and this is a definite break from the stereotype.
Moreover, Reid allows this departure from tradition not only to his
wild-west but also to his genteel characters. The entire burden of
The Quadroon lies in the right of the hero and heroine to unite
despite class and racial barriers.

Englishmen were very interested in their American distaff
cousins, as is apparent in the comments of British travellers and in
the rather feeble fictional attempts to depict American women.
There was a widespread belief that American girls were spoiled. As
Anthony Trollope put it in *He Knew He Was Right* (1869),
"American women are taught by the habits of their country to think
that men should give way to them more absolutely than is in accor-
dance with the practices of life in Europe." Yet British novelists
observed with amazement the independence of American girls living away from home. In *The Trial* (1864), Charlotte M. Yonge com-
mented about a young girl attending Columbia University and living an independent life in a New York boardinghouse just as her
male English counterpart might have done at an English university.
The independent American woman had a freedom quite startling to
English society. Anthony Trollope writes : "In America a girl may
form a friendly intimacy with any young man she fancies. . . . It is
her acknowledged right to enjoy herself after that fashion and to
have what she calls a good time with young men. . . . She goes
out to balls and picnics with them and afterwards lets herself in with
a latchkey, while her papa and mama are a-bed and asleep, with
perfect security."[10] Trollope's comments are particularly interesting
because he records, in an expository manner, precisely the same
freedoms Reid depicts symbolically and romantically.

Certainly Reid admired what he believed to be the equality of American women. And because of his political biases, he saw this equality as a benefit for society as a whole as well as for the specific love relationship. Reid describes Virginia Randolph, sister of the gentleman-hero of *Oçeola*, as having developed a "feeling of perfect independence, which, among American women, is common enough, but, in other lands can only exist among those of the privileged classes. . . . She was independent . . . her fortune was her own. In the States of America, the law of entail is not allowed" (pp. 268 - 69), and thus no oligarchy can be created.

Yet despite their independence and autonomy, most of Mayne Reid's heroines are young—some extremely so. As we have noted earlier, Zöe of *Scalp Hunters* is only twelve when the hero falls in love with her, while Blanche Vernon, the heroine of *Child Wife*, is but thirteen. In part this follows the tradition of the sentimental novels of the period whose very young heroines may have been related to Victorian social mores which placed a high value on virginity. But Reid's choice of such heroines also is closely related to his own experiences with women and to his travels in southern America. He accounts for Zöe's eligibility on the basis of geography, for "she was the child of a sunny clime; and I had often seen at that age, under the warm sky of Mexico, the wedded bride, the fond mother" (p. 86).

Apart from their autobiographical interest and their traditional role in the sentimental novel, Reid's young heroines challenge psychological interpretation. Cooper's Inez de Certavallos (*The Prairie*, 1827) is easily taken for a child and in his study, *The Romance in America* (Middletown, Conn., 1969), Joel Porte suggests that Inez represents "an additional fillip of nymphet sexuality recurrent in our literature from Poe to Nabokov" and that her youthfulness turns her "in the direction of a fantasy figure of pure carnality" (p. 43). Such a reading supports Harriet Martineau's analysis of the essentially inferior position of women in America, for these heroines are totally dominated by the adventure hero. As infantile characters they are incapable of autonomous behavior and must depend on the superiority of the heroes. Thus Reid's Lillian Holt spends her time (often even in situations of great peril) languishing and writing puerile poetry telling her lord, "I think [only] of thee" (*Wild Huntress*, p. 190), while Zöe, who knows not (at the age of twelve) the meaning of the word, ask her lover in a trembling voice "what is 'to marry?'" (p. 93). Henry Haller's greatest pleasure at the end of the novel is the thought of "that promised hour when I am to teach, and *she* to learn, '*what is to marry*'" (p. 378). Yet much as he idealizes these innocent, dependent heroines and seemingly approves of their being dominated by the manly heroes, Reid also shows great admiration for such strong female characters as Marian Holt and Eugénie Besançon.

The primary attraction about love in America was its freedom, and for Reid this is often made manifest in a preference for his dark-haired masculine heroines whom he often describes as mustachioed. They have a "faint dark tracing on the upper lip" that holds a peculiar fascination for him. This may be an emblem of their freedom, for with the addition of some male qualities they become capable of living up to the potential for freedom offered by America. These women often ride astride "à la Duchesse de Berri" as Reid puts it in one of his admiring descriptions. They sometimes demonstrate skill in handling the lasso and often, as is the case with Marian Holt, they are expert shots. Yet they are also tender, loving women, unafraid to declare their love as well as to fight for it.

Reid never resolves the dichotomy of these feminine characters. As hero-author he prefers young, submissive heroines; as radical-author he admires strong, egalitarian heroines. Attempting to work his way out of the ambivalence between English and American views of women and the reality and fantasy of his own life, Reid comes to the point where he can allow his gentlemen heroes to marry the strong, autonomous, even masculine women he has created. This is certainly the case with Catalina de Cruces (*White Chief*) and Adela Miranda (*Lone Ranche*). Perhaps the increasing importance and value given to the masculine-independent heroines was a function of Reid's own choice of marrying a Zöe/Lillian "child bride" whom he could control and who would worship him unquestioningly. Perhaps his political-philosophical fantasy was ahead of its time; certainly his choice of a wife was sanctioned both by his society and by his own ego—one that demanded support and sustenance. Had he remained in the United States and become a successful Santa Fe trader or the literary figure of his dreams, his choice of a wife might have been different. As it happens, his fictional "wives" become more and more unlike his real one.

These observations are not intended to attach any great value to the love plots of the romances. Essentially they are purest melodrama. Yet in the depiction of his women, Reid develops a major theme: love conquers because American women are free and independent and American institutions (unlike their English counterparts) will not hamper the course of true love. These conditions cause Reid to depart from the tradition Richardson established in *Pamela* of having the woman break class barriers through marriage—a convention deriving in part from the expectations of a largely middle-class feminine audience. As many, if not most of Mayne Reid's readers were men, and because he is writing out his own fantasy life, Reid reverses the formula to allow his heroes to rise through marriage. At times he even surmounts the materialistic view of marriage to present a situation of total equality wherein two independent and autonomous persons join hands and hearts to create a new family that usually represents what Reid perceived as the social and philosophical ideals of America.

IV Wish-fulfillment in Popular Fiction

The popularity of a given literary genre and of a particular author may be ascertained from such statistics as book sales, subscription lists, and numbers of editions, but an understanding of the reasons underlying popular taste depends on less tangible evidence, primarily upon psychological theory. Especially when dealing with popular literature, the critic cannot appeal to traditional aesthetics and must therefore look elsewhere for an explanation of the powerful appeal of such works.

Ian Watt has remarked that the novel has a power over the consciousness that makes possible its "role as the purveyor of vicarious sexual experience and adolescent wish-fulfillment" regardless of the literary quality of the work in question (p. 204). If this statement holds true for the novel, closely grounded in the manners and mores of real life, how much more valid it is for the romance, with its greater emphasis on fantasy. And the importance of fulfilling wish-dreams can hardly be overemphasized. Mayne Reid, in an effort to accomplish this without being false to British reality, usually transported his characters to the New World, where he had first transported himself and where he created a world that was part factual and part purely imaginary. The *Spectator*, taking cognizance of this duality in Reid's work, defended the prevalence of violence in his books because "the author knew his scenes of murder, vengeance and torture to be true, and felt them to be as much beyond his power to alter as the tropical vegetation." The reviewer went on to analyze the underlying significance of his work: "It is to be rid of the coercing, compressing, and therefore limiting chain of cause and effect,—to set the imagination really free, and let it revel for a moment in an unconditioned world. It does revel, and we all like the momentary sensation, even though we are all the while critical enough to be annoyed with our own pleasure" (October 27, 1883, p. 1375). We all are aware of the limitations of individual human experience, governed not only by the "limiting chain of cause and effect" but also by the spatial and temporal nature of life. Man has an innate desire to expand such limitations as best he can, faced as he is with the knowledge of ultimate death, with the imperfect nature of the world in which he lives, with a desire for love and admiration. Above all, as Simon O. Lesser states, "man is an indefatigable seeker of pleasure. If human experience does not yield enough satisfaction . . . he will strive at least . . . to create other worlds more in accord with his desires."[11] And one of the ways that man has been able to achieve such pleasurable expansion has been by reading fiction. Although it may be true that popular fiction requires little introspection or self-analysis on the part of the reader, it may still serve a valuable purpose. Even Q. D. Leavis, who deplores the usual level of popular taste, admits that "fantasy-fiction is the typical reading of a people whose normal impulses are starved of the means of expression."[12] And such readers will often make use of the analogizing feature of the human mind in order to derive significance from a work that has no apparent relevance to their own lives. Victorian readers of Mayne Reid's American tales did not all expect to go to America and live Mayne Reid's fantasies, and yet there can be little doubt that they projected the freedom and success of his characters in America into their own lives at home.

The main restriction in Mayne Reid's wish-fulfillment fantasies originates from the same source as the undeniable power of his fiction: his dependence on the repetition of the autobiographical pattern. Reid's imagination limits him to the single dream of himself as liberated hero in America. All the novels repeat this pattern, either explicitly or implicitly. Thus the only identification that Reid's audience can make depends upon the facility with which they appropriate Reid's projected self-image, for Reid was always limited in his fictional creations to those drawn from his own experiences, real or imaginary. This autobiographical emphasis naturally limits the psychological complexity of his works, but at the same time makes them suitable to readers of popular fiction discussed above.

One test of art in fiction is the ability of the author to transform the raw materials of his personal experience so that they recur in different patterns. The raw materials of the life of any writer remain the same, and the only possibility for theme and variation comes from the power of his imagination to project them in different guises. Thus both *David Copperfield* and *Great Expectations* may be considered as "autobiographical" novels although neither has an exact correspondence to Dickens's life, and the later novel works out Dickens's autobiographical experiences at a more sophisticated psychological level than the earlier. In the case of D. H. Lawrence a similar pattern appears as he moves from the rather literally autobiographical *Sons and Lovers* to the imaginative transfer of later novels like *The Rainbow* (where many of the dreams and aspirations of the masculine author are adapted to his feminine heroine) and to the fragmentation of personality in *Women in Love*. Such great writers express personal and universal desires with an artistic complexity that is completely lacking in Reid, who retells endlessly the same American adventure with which he was obsessed.

Three main aspects of Reid's work deserve psychological consideration: the adventure tale itself, the violence and fear endemic to its plot, and the role of sex in the lives of its characters. Q. D. Leavis might have been describing Reid's adventure tales rather than such twentieth-century popular novels as *The Desert Dreamers, Lure of the Desert*, and *The Golden Journey*, which she describes as specializing "in fantasy-spinning" with heroes who are prone to such speeches as " 'I thought we should go together, man and mate, out into the wide, clean spaces of the world, and build our life there as men and women have done before, and make a big thing of it.' " This, says Mrs. Leavis, "is a fair specimen of the kind of fiction classed as day-dreaming" (p. 54). Mrs. Leavis takes the moral position that such ideas expressed in such tales are reprehensible, and yet they are universal human tendencies. We might wish to find them in literature of a higher artistic quality, but the universality of the day-dreaming function has been recognized by Freud, who related it to the creative impulse itself and felt that it could be observed best in the work of "popular" rather than "great" artists. Of such works he wrote: "They all have a hero who is the centre of interest, for whom the author tries to win our sympathy by every possible means. . . . If at the end of one chapter the hero is left unconscious and bleeding from severe wounds, I am sure to find him at the beginning of the next . . . on the road to recovery. . . . This significant mark of invulnerability very closely betrays His Majesty the Ego, the hero of all day-dreams and all novels."[13]

Freud's daydream is the "ego-trip" that readers of Mayne Reid know so well. The heroine always succumbs to the hero's superiority, the most evil villains are overcome, the malignity of society falls away, and "they live happily ever after." Reading such fiction can be satisfying psychologically, for while evil is punished inexorably, chance and good luck so frequently work on the side of the hero as to validate Simon Lesser's claim that popular fiction can satisfy ambitious or erotic desires (p. 98). But before Elysium can be reached, the hero must engage in a series of tests, most of which, psychologically speaking, serve alternately to generate and to allay the reader's anxiety. As Lesser describes it, this fiction gives pleasure by exploiting "the satisfaction we secure from dealing with anxiety under controlled conditions which assure its eventual liquidation. . . . Our attention is distracted from our anxieties themselves to an enjoyable way of dealing with them. The heroes of this kind of fiction have to face obstacles and danger . . . robbed of much of their terror by the assurance—offered by the work or often a priori by the genre to which it belongs—that they will be overcome" (pp. 261 - 62). Living in a world full of anxieties to be faced daily, the readers of Mayne Reid's adventure tales could therefore displace some of their anxieties and tensions in the surrogate heroes of these tales and obtain a comforting release from anxiety, however impermanent and however negligible the literary merit of the work which inspired it.

V Violence, Repression, and Adventure

The generation of these fictional anxieties in Reid's works depends heavily on violence and fear, features common to many greater works. Indeed, Walter C. Phillips believes that the lesser novelists of the nineteenth century imitated Dickens, of whom he states that from *Oliver Twist* to *Edwin Drood* "there is no full-length story of his without its generous reliance upon the most brutal stimulants to fear."[14] Certainly Reid played upon the psychological possibilities of fear and terror. The *Spectator* noted that his works "positively smell of blood," mitigated only in part by their air of unreality. Reid uses melodrama to express the aggressive

tendencies, sexual and otherwise, that society demands be controlled in everyday life. His method shows his understanding of
both popular taste and psychology. In Reid's time the vogue for
Newgate novels was over with a public already too familiar with
crime and violence at home. By setting his deeds of terror in distant
lands, Reid could capitalize on the audience's ignorance as well as
on their interest both in the exotic and in the terrifying. For Reid,
the Indian becomes an agent to create as well as displace anxiety.
Thus from the abstract "whooping savages, horrid to behold" of
Wild Huntress (p. 248) to the concrete Comanches on the warpath
of *War Trail*, who are rumored to have "butchered the men as is
their wont, and carried off the women, children, and chattels" (p.
12), the Indian replaces the highwayman of an earlier period. The
terrible sufferings of Negro slavery replace the sufferings of the
English wage-slave or child laborer of the Victorian social novels.
And always there is terror in the very beauty of the western
landscape with its aspects of fearful strangeness—evident when the
narrator of *Scalp Hunters* describes his response to the "stupendous
cliffs" of the desert canyons as "a feeling of awe . . . and a
shuddering sensation" (p. 106).[15]

   In Reid's work the expression of fear and terror often finds release
in scenes with an extremely sadomasochistic quality. Certainly the
extreme purity of Reid's heroes and heroines is balanced by the
sadomasochistic rituals that often occur in his works. A particularly
graphic example of this appears when Edward Warfield, the
autobiographical hero of *Guerilla Chief*, argues with himself over
his "impure" motives and lustful feelings for the peasant maiden
Dolores. Later these nearly explicit sexual desires find release
through displacement as the evil guerilla band captures the girl,
strips her to her thin chemise, and nearly rapes her. Excerpts from
the scene make clear the psychological ramifications: "Evidently
some fiendish spectacle was at hand. . . . The girl was destined to
some atrocious treatment—some infamous exhibition! . . . They
appeared to be disrobing her, or rather tearing the clothes from her
back! . . . I saw that the only covering which concealed her person
from the lewd eyes that were gazing upon her, was a slight chemise
of thin cotton stuff, scarcely reaching to her knees. . . . A sort of
truck bedstead . . . was brought forth. . . . I saw him [the villain]
preparing for the grave deed. . . . Her cries were of themselves
sufficient to fill my heart with the acme of extreme bitterness" (pp.

114 - 16). The villain then escapes on horseback, "both arms en-
circling the semi-nude body" of the girl, who is rescued by the hero
and his friends only after an exciting mounted chase.

Other typical instances of sadomasochism are the female mutila-
tion (ear-amputation) of *War Trail* and the events of the chapter in
Wild Huntress entitled "A Captive on a Crucifix" when the heroes
are bound to crosses for the target practice of Indian villains, an
event that also occurs in *The Lost Mountain*. Sadomasochistic practices are most prevalent in *White Chief*, where they are reinforced
by the role played in the torture by priests. The following excerpt is
illustrative:

> The priests wore an official look. They were in the act of officiating. At
> what? Listen!
> The asses were mounted. On the back of each was a form—a human
> form. These sat not freely, but in constrained attitudes. . . .
> Both were nude to the waist, and below it. The eye needed but one
> glance at those forms to tell they were women! The long loose hair—in the
> one grey, in the other golden—shrouding their cheeks, and hanging over
> the necks of the animals, was further proof of this. For one it was not need-
> ed. The outlines were those of a Venus. A sculptor's eye could not have
> detected a fault. In the form of the other, age had traced its marks. . . .
> Oh, God! what a sight for the eye of Carlos the cibolero! Those involun-
> tary riders *were his mother and sister!* . . .
> These [the villains] with ready alacrity took up their cue, gathered the
> thick ends of their cuartos around their wrists, and plied the lash upon the
> naked backs of the women. The strokes were deliberate and mea-
> sured—they were counted! Each seemed to leave its separate wale upon the
> skin. Upon the younger female they were more conspicuous,—not that they
> had been delivered with greater severity, but upon the softer, whiter skin,
> the purple lines appeared plainer by contrast. (III, 169 - 72)

Carlos's mother dies as a result of the torture, and Carlos (who has
been forced to watch this exhibition in the village plaza from the
window of his prison cell) is naturally inspired with an impassioned
desire for revenge against the villains responsible—not only the
priests but also the Mexican military authorities they serve. This
kind of sadism derives from the gothic (and ultra-Protestant) school
insofar as it is connected with the "practices" of the Roman
Catholic Church. But more important than any school or source is
the psychological meaning behind such scenes being presented in a
novel published in 1855 in standard three-volume form at 31*s* 6*d*

and therefore intended for a respectable class of readers rather than the "penny-dreadful" trade.

The torture scene involving his mother and sister provides an excuse for Carlos himself to engage in sadistic behavior at the end of the novel when he gains his revenge by forcing his enemies, mounted on blindfolded horses, to leap from a high precipice to their deaths. On one level this scene appeals to the super-ego (the desire for control), but it is actually an example of what Lesser calls "tickling the id" by admitting surreptitiously "a great deal of instinctual gratification of a sado-masochistic nature. For example . . . a lynching . . . punishment is no more than an excuse for the release of hatred and vindictiveness" (p. 105). The fact that lynchings and attempted lynchings occur so frequently in Reid's novels comes in part from his western American settings; the gusto with which he describes them, however, leads to speculation that he uses them for such purposes as Lesser suggests.

Steven Marcus has shown the presence and importance of pornography in the Victorian Age,[16] and in some respects the torture scene described above is very close to pornography, as it substitutes violence and pain for normal sexual arousal. Although the pursuit of woman is omnipresent in Reid's novels, contact between men and women is kept to a tender kiss or an abstractly described "passionate embrace"; the intimate physical aspects of sexual passion are never delineated in anything like the descriptive detail of the scenes of violence. In works that repeat endlessly the same patterns of violence such as the stampede, the duel or ambush, and the chase, it is possible to see an analogy to the patterns of pornography present for example in the notorious Victorian work, *My Secret Life*, whose author does not understand why he always wants to repeat his experiences. According to Marcus, "sexuality in this conception consists of an endless accumulation of experiences . . . both different and the same" (p. 181). The experiences of the anonymous author of *My Secret Life* resemble the events in Reid's tales in that both represent extreme and sometimes violent activity for the satisfaction of deep but little understood psychological needs.

Thus such events in Reid's novels offer a release for repressed sexual activity; even in the asexual books Reid wrote strictly for boys, one can see the possibility of the omnipresent violence serving as a surrogate for sexuality. In any case, it is evident that readers who were attracted to this kind of fiction either lacked literary discrimination or were "so desperate for an anodyne," as Lesser puts it, that they overlooked its shortcomings for the satisfaction of a euphoric state depicted in shades of black and white containing hidden appeals to their deepest psychological nature.

A Victorian audience read Reid for his action-filled adventure stories, no doubt unconscious of the psychological implications that a twentieth-century critic discerns. Yet such underlying implications suggest that there is something in human psychology that responds to scenes of violence, to the lure of the unknown, and to the excitement of a sexual chase that must be experienced symbolically through art because it is not sanctioned by society.

CHAPTER 5

A *Twentieth-Century Perspective*

THE popular literature of one age rapidly becomes the
ephemeral and often obscure curiosity of another. What
survives the caprices of time and shifting taste is usually not the
most typical but the best. Thus Shakespeare's plays remain the
paramount achievement of the English Renaissance rather than the
works of Jonson or any number of lesser authors, while among the
myriad of Victorian novelists only a few—Dickens, Thackeray,
Eliot, Hardy—have endured. Similarly, Thomas Mayne Reid, one
of the most prolific writers of his own or any other age, has faded
into nearly total obscurity since his death in 1883. During his
lifetime Reid's name and his works were common household words,
although even then his work enjoyed varying popularity that took
him from prosperity to bankruptcy and halfway back again. In the
long term, like most writers of popular fiction, his reputation was
short-lived.

Despite Reid's failure to gain a lasting place in belles lettres, his
works are more than mere literary curiosities or subjects for scholarly inquiry. Reid's particular combination of factual detail, escapist
fiction, and radical politics creates particular effects atypical of his
period. Written during the political ferment of the Victorian Age,
Reid's novels help us to understand and to interpret those times.
For while Reid's limited imagination ultimately may have failed
him, his politics transcend the narrow prescriptions of his genre and
link him to a long line of writers who have always rebelled against
the oppression and enslavement of mankind. In this Reid is especially linked to the Romantic Age and most specifically to Byron,
who exemplified for Reid the proper relationship between an
author, his literature, and his society. But Reid was no less in sympathy with Blake or Rousseau, who looked around them and saw
that mankind was "everywhere in chains."

Beyond the radical politics in his writing, what distinguishes Reid

131

from the mainstream of Victorian popular fiction are his precise American settings and his attention to scientific detail. While Reid does not limit his fictional settings to America, his imagination often returned there. Unfortunately, his youthful experiences soon prescribed the limits of his fiction. Initially, Reid converted his own adventures into fantastic, flamboyant tales that revolve around a thinly disguised autobiographical hero. Such stories frequently strain the boundaries of credibility, and his later works were subject to further distortion and elaborate fantasy. A cursory look at Reid's biography shows a confused relationship between fact and fiction that we inevitably suspect was Reid's own.

In spite of their bizarre plots and biographical convolutions, a consistent vision of America informs Reid's novels and juvenile fictions. America was always far more than the mere subtext of Reid's tales; it was a symbol for change and freedom in a world that gradually was demolishing the strictures of age-old despotism. Reid's work is a potpourri of two of the most popular literary elements of his day: the travel book and the adventure romance. In his best works these elements fuse and forge an idealized and expansive vision of the American West. The popularity of his work helped to imprint that particular image of America on a host of readers throughout the world. Reid's respect and admiration for American political and social institutions led him to depict them as viable alternatives to the oppression he perceived in England and Europe. Reid's impression of America corresponds to that presented by Sir Rose Lambart Price in his travel book *The Two Americas* (London: Sampson Low, 1877): "The future greatness of the American nation will undoubtedly come from the West; and without having been West, an individual, no matter how far-sighted and deep thinking he may imagine himself, will fail, not only in grasping whence the real wealth and prosperity of the nation must eventually be derived, but where also already much of the primary causes of success and contentment exist in a degree not to be met with in Europe" (pp. 345 - 46).

Reid took his readers West, although life in America was never so exciting as it appears on the feverishly adventurous pages of a Mayne Reid romance. And despite their factual bases, Reid's books would have been poor "emigrant guides" except possibly for students of natural history. But it is not always what is true but what people believe to be true that controls their destiny, and Mayne Reid's enthusiastic portrayal of America conveyed something beyond facts—a perception of possibility. Other British travel books may have offered accurate pictures of American life, but they lacked the intense commitment, the sense of poetic vision found in Reid's pages. And as that most astute of foreign travelers in America, Alexis de Tocqueville, observed in *Democracy in America:* "Nothing conceivable is so petty, so insipid, so anti-poetic as the life of a man in the United States. But among the thoughts which it suggests, there is always one that is full of poetry, and this is the hidden nerve which gives vigor to the whole frame. . . . In democratic ages the extreme fluctuations of men and the impatience of their desires keep them perpetually on the move so that the inhabitants of different countries intermingle, see, listen to, and borrow from each other" (1835; rpt. New York: Vintage, 1945, 2, 78 - 79).

Amid the fluctuations of his time, Reid's pen played its part in intermingling the inhabitants of Britain and America, and if modern readers examine the romances Mayne Reid wrote about America and seek a glimpse of the "nerve which gives vigor to the whole frame" they will discover it to be Reid's passionate, though flawed, vision of the unity in diversity and the equality of all men that was the promise of America.

Most of what Reid wrote (including some twenty-seven novels, twenty-six juvenile books, bits of poetry, numerous articles and short stories) has long been out of print. A few copies gather dust in the research libraries of the world. But a new generation of readers may yet enjoy the fantastic tales of the captain who "fibs on a surprising scale" yet to whom we listen because he does so "with the finish of an artist." Significantly, three Reid works, *Boy Hunters,* *White Chief,* and *The Quadroon,* have been included among the titles reprinted in fascimile for the Gregg Press "Americans in Fiction" Series. According to the prospectus, these books were selected as "indispensable to the study and understanding of American social and literary history, culture, and folkways." The choice of Reid as such an interpreter validates the premise of this book that his was a deep and perceptive understanding of the country that was first in his heart even though he lived only twelve of his sixty-five years there. Romantic, idealistic, escapist though he was, when he wrote of America he wrote his best. Back in England, he longed to return, and failing that he returned in his imagination to this land of his "affectionate longings." Mayne Reid's life and works reveal the intense power of nineteenth-century America as a shaping force

on those who came to her shores. America gave Reid substantiation
for his youthful idealism and the material for a literary career
seldom equalled in terms of sheer productivity. Reid repaid his debt
to America, for in his romances he captured many of the now
vanished characters of the Old West, details of a wilderness gone
forever, and the spirit of freedom when many were enslaved.

Notes and References

Chapter One

1. Reid's life has been shrouded in obscurity and misinformation because all authorites have relied upon the original published sources, which depend very heavily on Reid's own lively imagination. The earliest published information appears in *Men of the Time: Biographical Sketches of Eminent Living Characters* (London: Kent, 1859). Reid, who was then at the height of his fame, must have supplied the information for the entry, but it does not correlate with that to be found in either of his widow's biographies, *Mayne Reid: A Memoir of His Life* (London: Ward & Downey, 1890) or *Captain Mayne Reid: His Life and Adventures* (London: Greening, 1900), a work in which Elizabeth Reid was assisted by an American, Charles H. Coe. The Reid-Ollivant papers, now in possession of Queen's University, Belfast, provide little biographical information. They consist of a biographical sketch and some observations about Captain and Mrs. Reid's family life by a niece, Helen Cromie Mollan; 318 letters dated 1865 to 1883 written by Reid to his private secretary, Charles Ollivant; and Ollivant's holograph manuscript for a biography of Reid. These materials were plagiarized by Mrs. Reid for her works. A version of Ollivant's manuscript was published serially in *Uses: A New Church Journal*, which also contains Ollivant's attack on Mrs. Reid for misusing his manuscript, and correspondence from Charles H. Coe regarding the controversy. The Reid-Ollivant papers also disclose some biographical facts of minor importance such as Elizabeth Reid's distate for everything American that her husband so admired and Reid's apparent addiction to opiates to ease the pain resulting from his serious illness in later life.

2. Elizabeth Reid and Charles H. Coe, *Captain Mayne Reid: His Life and Adventures* (London: Greening, 1900), pp. 9 - 12. Characteristically, Mrs. Reid has Audubon accompanying her husband, when the reverse would be more likely. All future citations in the text refer to this work.

3. "Recollections of Edgar Allen [sic] Poe," *Munsey's Magazine*, 7 (August 1892), 555 - 56.

4. The series continued as follows: "The Action of Molino del Rey" and "The Storming of Chapultepec" (December 11, p. 489); "The Battle of Churubusco," "The Great Battle of Mexico," and "The Taking of Contreras" (December 18, pp. 507 - 09). The dates of these campaigns were: Vera Cruz, March 9 - 29, 1847; Contreras and Churubusco, August 19 - 20; Molino del Rey, September 8; Chapultepec, September 13. Mexico City fell to American forces September 14, 1847.

5. *Fun*, 4 (September 5, 1863), 241. At the first meeting of the "Company" *Fun* reports, "Captain Mayne Reid said . . . that men never tired of those distant prairies where the *felis domesticus* (or common cat) listened to the wail—" The parody of Reid appeared in *Fun*, 5 (September 19, 1863), 4 - 7.

6. *American Thanksgiving Day Dinner* (London: Wm. Ridgeway, 1863), pp. 70 - 75. Although Mrs. Reid states that her husband became an American citizen during his second visit to the United States, there is no record of his naturalization.

7. Pierpont Morgan Library; Ticknor Papers, Library of Congress. The Reid novels issued by De Witt from 1858 - 68 were: *Wood-Rangers; Wild Life; Osceola; The Maroon; Tiger-Hunter; Wild Huntress;* and *Headless Horseman*. *Wood-Rangers* and *Tiger-Hunter* were translations from Louis de Bellemare. Except for *Wild Life* there is no doubt about the authenticity of the other titles. The issue is further clouded because of the publishing history of *Tiger-Hunter*. This novel was published in French as *Costal l'Indien, roman historique* (Paris: V. Lecou, 1852), and appeared in an English translation as *Costal, the Indian Zapotec* (London: James Blackwood, 1857). Its next appearance was as *A Hero in Spite of Himself*, translated by Captain Mayne Reid (London: Hurst & Blackett, 1861). Finally Bellemare's authorship disappears in the title, *The Tiger-Hunter, or; a Hero in Spite of Himself* (New York: Carleton, 1874). The title page of this last edition reads "first published, 1865." The last two books are identical.

8. The *Onward* bibliography cannot be explicated here. However, many of the entries are Reid's old writings. Two examples are representative. The poem "I Think of Thee" (*Onward*, 1 [January 1869], 24) first appeared in *Wild Huntress* (London, 1861), while *Croquet*, a book of rules for the game, had been published in England in 1863. Moreover, a comparison of the two versions of "Croquet" shows the *Onward* version to be prolix and redundant.

9. Autograph letter (January 6, 1876) to Isaac Latimer of the *Western Daily Mercury* (Fales Collection, New York Univ. Libraries).

10. Reid's letter was printed in the Boston *Evening Transcript* on March 24, 1884 (p. 6).

Chapter Two

1. *The Rise of the Novel: Studies in Defoe, Richardson, and Fielding* (1957; rpt. Berkeley: Univ. of California Press, 1964), p. 15.

2. *Anatomy of Criticism* (Princeton, N.J.: Princeton Univ. Press, 1957), p. 186.

3. *Studies in Classic American Literature* (1923; rpt. New York: Viking, 1964), p. 51.

4. *War Life*, an extremely rare title, not held by the Library of Congress or the British Museum, was discovered by the author in 1970

through correspondence with the University of Texas Library. The title page reads, "New York: Printed by A. J. Townsend, 'Literary American' Press."

5. *Spirit of the Times* (December 11, 1847), p. 109. Reid often builds upon this kind of description to evoke a vicarious sense of danger in his audience. Cf. "You live in a northern zone, in a land of pools and streams and limpid springs. You have never felt thirst. You know not the want of water" (*Scalp Hunters*, p. 67).

6. In *Rifle Rangers*, Reid began his practice of commenting on such matters in lengthy notes that cover every possible exoticism from the pronunciation of Spanish to the preparation of Mexican food. In the comparison that follows, quotations from *Rifle Rangers* are taken from the English first edition as the most authoritative text for establishing shifts in style and content important to the genesis under discussion. Because of the proliferation of editions and the inaccessibility of first editions, it has not been possible to follow this practice consistently for all the works cited herein.

7. "The Western Fiction of Mayne Reid," *Western American Literature*, 3 (Autumn 1968), 117 - 18. Of course, such a précis would describe much mid-nineteenth-century popular fiction that was characterized by a blending of sensationalism and sentimentality.

8. *Cooper's Americans* (Columbus: Ohio State Univ. Press, 1965), p. 205.

9. Garey is identified in "The W. M. Boggs Manuscript about Bent's Fort, Kit Carson, the Far West and Life Among the Indians," ed. Le Roy R. Hafen, *Colorado Magazine*, 7 (March 1930), 49. See also George B. Grinnell, "Bent's Old Fort and Its Builders," Kansas State Historical Society *Collections*, 15 (1919), 28 - 91. Helen Cromie Mollan's manuscript asserts that Reid knew Garey.

10. *The Literary Emancipation of a Region: The Changing Image of the American West in Fiction* (Ann Arbor, Mich.: University Microfilms, 1957), p. 134.

11. Reid's Ichabod Crane variation—seemingly so derivative and fantastic—may have a more solid biographical foundation, for in *Tales of Old-Time Texas* (Boston: Little Brown [1955]), James Frank Dobie points out the prevalence of headless horseman legends at the time Mayne Reid is believed to have been in Texas. See "The Headless Horseman of the Mustangs," pp. 147 - 54.

12. In a letter to Dr. J. S. Crone, quoted in "Captain Mayne Reid, Soldier and Novelist," *The Northern Whig*, November 14, 1905. I am indebted to Dr. and Mrs. E. Mayne Reid for supplying me with this and other ephemeral source materials.

13. *The Savages of America: A Study of the Indian and the Idea of Civilization* (Baltimore: Johns Hopkins, 1953), p. 6.

14. *The Year of Decision: 1846* (New York: Houghton Mifflin, 1962), p. 404. However, although he is certainly quite gothic, Seguin is neither "prettified" nor the hero of the romance.

15. Osceola denied having white blood and "repeatedly and scornfully repudiated the name 'Powell' " according to Charles H. Coe, *Red Patriots* (Cincinnati: Editor, 1898), p. 28. On the other hand, twentieth-century scholarship indicates that Osceola's maternal great-grandfather was a Scot named McQueen.

16. Reid supposedly arrived in New Orleans aboard the *Dumfriesshire* January 16, 1840, and although he takes great pains to point out in the "Preface" that "the author is *not* the hero," the only name we know the hero by is the "travelling name" he assumes to outwit the villain. That name is his mother's maiden name of Rutherford, which was the maiden name of Reid's mother.

17. *Glances Back Through Seventy Years* (London: Kegan Paul, 1893). Vizetelly was not anxious to become involved in such dangerous affairs, even though Reid suggested the innocent ruse of dropping the passports in Lincoln's Inn Fields for a prearranged pickup. Vizetelly remarks, "I told the fire-eating captain that with every disposition to oblige him neither I nor Mr. Birket Foster would care to become marked individuals in the eyes of police authorities all over Europe" (I, 383 - 84).

Chapter Three

1. See *The English Common Reader* (Chicago: Univ. of Chicago Press, 1957), p. 388. Altick's statement that *Scalp Hunters* sold over a million copies in Great Britain in the forty years since its publication is based on Elizabeth Reid.

2. *Children's Books in England*, 2nd ed. (1958; rpt. Cambridge, England: Cambridge Univ. Press, 1966), p. 301.

3. ALS. Courtesy Houghton Library, Harvard Univ.

4. *Tales Out of School* (London: Heinemann, 1948), p. 4.

5. Preface to Cornelia Meigs, et al., *A Critical History of Children's Literature* (New York: Macmillan, 1953), pp. xiii - xiv.

6. For a general survey of the dime novel, see Edmund Pearson's *Dime Novels* (Boston: Little, Brown and Co., 1929). The best and most comprehensive study of these works and their authors is Albert Johannsen's *The House of Beadle and Adams and Its Dime and Nickel Novels*, 3 vols. (Norman: Univ. of Okla. Press, 1950).

7. See "The Dime Novel: Its Origin, Growth, and Influence. Reminiscences of Mayne Reid," *Boston Evening Transcript*, March 27, 1884, p. 6. I discuss here only *The White Squaw, The Yellow Chief*, and *The War Trail*. The first two titles were published in England in their dime-novel versions; *Wild Horse Hunters* and *The Planter Pirate* were not, while *The Helpless Hand* was reprinted in England as *The Fatal Cord*.

From Reid's many adult fictions also appearing in dime-novel form, I have chosen to discuss *The War Trail* because it is both a representative example and one available in both versions.

8. For a discussion of Moses ("Black") Harris, Ceran St. Vrain, and the mountain men of the Rocky Mountain fur trade, see Bernard De Voto, *Across the Wide Missouri* (Boston: Hougton Mifflin, 1947), *passim*.

9. "The Dime Novel," *Boston Evening Transcript* (March 27, 1884), *loc. cit.* Whittaker was himself a prolific writer of dime novels and collaborated with Reid on several books.

10. See "Dime Novels and the American Tradition," *Yale Review*, 26 (Summer 1937), 761.

Chapter Four

1. *Mudie's Select Library: Principal Works of Fiction in Circulation in 1848, 1858, 1869* (Ann Arbor, Mich.: Univ. Microfilms), 1955.

2. See Louis James, *Fiction for the Working Man, 1830 - 1850* (London: Oxford Univ. Press, 1963), p. 136. See also Graham Pollard's "Novels in Newspapers," *RES*, 18 (January 1942), 72 - 85. Pollard explores Reid's efforts to syndicate his novels in an attempt to increase his financial resources. *Gwen Wynn* (1877) was written expressly for syndication and has all the characteristics of such serial publication. Reid made it even more sensational by focusing the plot upon a scandal currently widely discussed in the daily press about Mary Jackson, an English girl imprisoned in a French convent.

3. For an illuminating study of the minor theaters and their relationships to both literature and the general society, see Maurice Willson Disher, *Blood and Thunder* (London: Frederick Muller Ltd., 1949).

4. The year before Reid's first English publication, the prominent radical journalist and barrister Alexander Mackay wrote *The Western World: or Travels in the United States*. Rated by Allan Nevins the best book of the period on America, it went through four British editions in 1850. For Nevins's discussion of this and other representative travel accounts, see *America Through British Eyes* (New York: Oxford Univ. Press, 1948). Max Berger, in what is probably an underestimate, states that about 230 American travel books were published by Englishmen in the years 1836 - 60. See *The British Traveller in America, 1836 - 1860* (New York: Columbia Univ. Press, 1943), p. 190.

5. Brightfield's article, "America and the Americans, 1840 - 1860, as Depicted in English Novels of the Period," *American Literature* 31 (November 1959), 309 - 24, provides an interesting examination of the Anglo-American literary scene. The passage quoted here is from p. 323.

6. John Norcross writes of *White Chief*: "Back of the tale, which is one of terror, there surely lies a solid base of fact, for such ruined towns have been discovered, abandoned by their former inhabitants. . . . It must

have gratified him [Reid] in his old age to have been so well vindicated by the results of exploration and the opening up of the country" (*New York Times*, November 11, 1905, p. 766, col. 1). In *Mesa, Cañon and Pueblo* (New York, 1924), another American expert, Charles F. Lummis, testified that "no one has ever been able to pick a serious flaw in Mayne Reid's history, geography, ethnology, or Zöology,—in fact his local color" (p. 16).

7. *Emigration and Disenchantment* (Norman: Univ. of Oklahoma Press, 1965), pp. 11 - 12.

8. *The American Adam* (Chicago: Univ. of Chicago Press, 1955), p. 5.

9. *The Tales of D. H. Lawrence* (London: Heinemann, 1934), p. 438.

10. The Trollope quotations apppear in Brightfield, pp. 311, 319.

11. *Fiction and the Unconscious* (1957; rpt. New York: Vintage, 1962), p. 21.

12. *Fiction and the Reading Public* (London: Chatto and Windus, 1932), p. 209.

13. "The Relation of the Poet to Day-Dreaming," *Character and Culture* (New York: Collier, 1963), p. 40.

14. *Dickens, Reade, and Collins: Sensation Novelists* (New York: Columbia Univ. Press, 1919), p. 49.

15. Cf. "White men have probably never felt so bitter anywhere, as here in America, where the very landscape, in its very beauty, seems a bit devilish and grinning, opposed to us," D. H. Lawrence, *Studies in Classic American Literature*, p. 56.

16. *The Other Victorians* (New York: Basic Books, 1966).

Selected Bibliography

PRIMARY SOURCES

This bibliography is limited to Reid's fictional titles published in book form. Entries are English first editions unless otherwise noted. Juvenile titles are so indicated. For the full bibliography of the canon, see Steele, "Mayne Reid: A Revised Bibliography," below.

War Life: or, The Adventures of a Light Infantry Officer. New York: A. J. Townsend, 1849. The first version of *Rifle Rangers.*

The Rifle Rangers: or, Adventures of an Officer in Southern Mexico. 2 vols. London: W. Shoberl, 1850. Illustrated. A later edition (London: J. C. Brown, c. 1860), has twelve illustrations by William Harvey engraved by Evans.

The Scalp Hunters: or, Romantic Adventures in Northern Mexico. 3 vols. London: Skeet, 1851.

The Desert Home: or, The Adventures of a Lost Family in the Wilderness. London: D. Bogue, 1852. Also published under the title *The English Family Robinson.* Juvenile.

The Boy Hunters: or, Adventures in Search of a White Buffalo. London: D. Bogue, 1853. Illustrated by William Harvey. Juvenile. Reprinted as part of the "Americans in Fiction" series with a Memoir by R. H. Stoddard. Ridgewood, N.J.: Gregg Press, 1968.

The Young Voyageurs: or, The Boy Hunters in the North. London: D. Bogue, 1854. Twelve illustrations by William Harvey. Juvenile.

The Forest Exiles: or, The Perils of a Peruvian Family Amid the Wilds of the Amazon. London: D. Bogue, 1854. Juvenile.

The Hunter's Feast: or, Conversations Around the Camp Fire. London: n.p. [1855].

The White Chief: A Legend of Northern Mexico. 3 vols. London: D. Bogue, 1855. Reprinted as part of the "Americans in Fiction" Series with original designs engraved by N. Orr. Ridgewood, N.J.: Gregg Press, 1968.

The Bush Boys: or, The History and Adventures of a Cape Farmer and His Family in the Wild Karoos of Southern Africa. London: D. Bogue, 1855. Juvenile.

The Young Yägers: or, A Narrative of Hunting Adventures in Southern Africa. London: D. Bogue, 1856. Juvenile.

The Quadroon: or, A Lover's Adventures in Louisiana. 3 vols. London:

Hyde, 1856. Rpt. New York: De Witt, 1856. Illustrated. Also published under the title *Love's Vengeance*. Reprinted as part of the "Americans in Fiction" Series with twelve illustrations by William Harvey, engraved by Evans. Ridgewood, N.J.: Gregg Press, 1967.

The Plant Hunters: or, Adventures Among the Himalaya Mountains. London: Ward and Lock, 1857. Rpt. Boston: Ticknor and Fields, 1866. Edmund Evans engravings. Juvenile.

The War Trail: or, The Hunt of the Wild Horse. London: n.p., 1857. Rpt. London: Routledge, Warne, & Routledge, 1860. William Harvey illustrations engraved by Edmund Evans. Beadle and Adams version dated November 22, 1882.

Ran Away to Sea: An Autobiography for Boys. London: Brown, 1858. It is not autobiographical. Juvenile.

Oçeola. 3 vols. London: Hurst and Blackett, 1859. Illustrated. Rpt. *Osceola: or, The Red Fawn of the Flower Land*. New York: Carleton, 1875. Another English edition under the title *The Half Blood*. London: Chapman and Hall [1861].

The Boy Tar: or, A Voyage in the Dark. London: W. Kent, 1859. Illustrated. Juvenile.

The Wood Rangers. (From the French of Louis de Bellemare.) By Captain Mayne Reid. 3 vols. London: Hurst and Blackett, 1860. [Bellemare's work was *Le Courer des Bois*. Paris: 1856.] Frontispiece to each volume drawn by J. B. Zwecker, engraved by Evans.

The Wild Huntress. 3 vols. London: R. Bentley, 1861. Also published as *Wild Huntress: or, The Big Squatter's Vengeance*. New York: Beadle and Adams, 1882.

Despard the Sportsman. London: H. Lea, 1861.

Bruin: or, The Grand Bear Hunt. London: Routledge, 1861. Juvenile.

A Hero in Spite of Himself. (From the French of L. de Bellemare.) By Captain Mayne Reid. [A free translation of "Costal l'Indien."] 3 vols. London: Hurst and Blackett, 1861. Reprinted as *The Tiger - Hunter*, London: C. H. Clarke, 1862.

The Maroon. 3 vols. London: Hurst and Blackett, 1862. Appeared serially in *Cassell's Illustrated Family Paper*, May 31 - July 19, 1862.

The Cliff Climbers: or, The Lone Home in the Himalayas. London: Ward and Lock, 1864. A sequel to *Plant Hunters*. Juvenile.

Ocean Waifs. London: D. Bryce, 1864. Sequel to *Ran Away to Sea*. Juvenile.

The White Gauntlet: A Romance. 3 vols. London: Skeet, 1864.

The Boy Slaves. London: C. H. Clarke, 1865. Rpt. London: Dent, 1928, with Introduction by Guy N. Pocock. Still in print in 1955. Juvenile.

The Headless Horseman: A Strange Tale of Texas. 2 vols. London: Chapman and Hall (Vol. 1), R. Bentley (Vol. 2), 1865. Illustrated.

The Bandolero: or, A Marriage Among the Mountains. London: R. Bentley, 1866. Also published as *The Mountain Marriage*. London [1867].

The Giraffe Hunters. 3 vols. London: Hurst and Blackett, 1867. A sequel to *Bush Boys* and *Young Yägers.* Juvenile.

The Guerilla Chief: And Other Tales. London: Darton, 1867. Eight Edmund Evans engravings. Contents: "Guerilla Chief," "Despard the Sportsman," "A Case of Retaliation," "The Broken Bitt," "A Turkey Hunt in Texas," "Trapped in a Tree," and "The Black Jaguar."

Afloat in the Forest. London: n.p., [1868]. American edition titled *Afloat in the Forest: A Voyage Among the Treetops.* Boston: Ticknor and Fields, 1867. Illustrated. Juvenile.

The Child Wife: A Tale of the Two Worlds. London: Ward and Lock, 1868.

The Planter Pirate: A Souvenir of the Mississippi. New York: Beadle and Adams, 1868. Reprinted as *The Land Pirates: or, The League of Devil's Island, A Tale of the Mississippi.* New York: Beadle and Adams, 1879.

The Helpless Hand: or, Backwoods Retribution. New York: Beadle and Adams, 1868. Reprinted as *The Fatal Cord: A Tale of Backwoods Retribution.* London: C. Brown, 1869. Juvenile.

The Castaways: A Story of Adventure in the Wilds of Borneo. London: T. Nelson, 1870. Juvenile.

The White Squaw and the Yellow Chief. London: C. H. Clarke, 1871. *White Squaw* first issued New York: Beadle and Adams [1868]. "Yellow Chief: A Romance of the Rocky Mountains" first appeared in *Onward*, 1 (January - June 1869), then in New York as Beadle and Adams's Dime Novel No. 189 (1869). It later appeared as *Blue Dick: or, The Yellow Chief's Vengeance.* New York: Beadle and Adams, 1879.

The Lone Ranche: A Tale of the 'Staked Plain.' 2 vols. London: Chapman and Hall, 1871.

The Finger of Fate: A Romance. 2 vols. London: Chapman, 1872. Also published in *Beeton's Boys' Annual for 1869.* Reprinted as *The Star of Empire: A Romance.* London: J. & R. Maxwell, [1888]. Juvenile.

The Cuban Patriot: or, The Beautiful Creole. An Episode of the Cuban Revolution. New York: Beadle and Adams, 1873.

The Death Shot: A Romance of Forest and Prairie. 3 vols. London: Chapman and Hall, 1873. Also, *The Death Shot: A Story Retold.* London: Ward, Lock and Tyler, 1874.

The Flag of Distress: A Story of the South Seas. 3 vols. London: W. Tinsley, 1876. First published in *Chambers's Journal*, 1875. A revised and expanded version of *Specter Barque.*

Gwen Wynn: A Romance of the Wye. 3 vols. London: Tinsley Bros., 1877.

The Wild-Horse Hunters. (With Frederick Whittaker.) New York: Beadle and Adams, [1877].

Gaspar the Gaucho: A Tale of the Gran Chaco. London: Routledge, 1879. A revised and expanded version of the unfinished "The Lost Sister."

Onward, 1 - 2 (January - December 1869), 1 - 10, 87 - 100, 181 - 92, 267 - 75, 357 - 67, 447 - 55; 38 - 46, 153 - 60, 185 - 91, 347 - 51, 370 - 74, 466 - 70.

The Specter Barque: A Tale of the Pacific. New York: Beadle and Adams, 1879. An abridged version of *Flag of Distress*. The first seven chapters are based on "The Stricken Crew." *Onward*, 3 (January 1870), 71 - 78.

The Queen of the Lakes: A Romance of the Mexican Valley. London: W. Mullan, 1880. Also published as *The Captain of the Rifles: or, The Queen of the Lakes*. New York: Beadle and Adams, 1879.

Cris Rock: or, A Lover in Chains. New York: R. Bonner [1889]. "Entered according to Act of Congress . . . 1879." The first version of *Free Lances*.

The Free Lances: A Romance of the Mexican Valley. 3 vols. London: Remington, 1881. A revised and expanded version of *Cris Rock*.

The Chase of Leviathan: or, Adventures in the Ocean. London: Routledge, 1885. Also published as *The Ocean Hunters: or, The Chase of Leviathan. A Romance of Perilous Adventure*. New York: Beadle and Adams, 1881. Juvenile.

The Vee-Boers: A Tale of Adventure in Southern Africa. London: Routledge [1885]. Elizabeth Reid says this was written in 1882 for the Boston periodical *Youth's Companion (Captain Mayne Reid*, p. 239). Juvenile.

The Land of Fire: A Tale of Adventure. London: Warne, [1884]. Serialized in *St. Nicholas*, 11 (December 1883 - May 1884), 160 - 67, 246 - 52, 309 - 19, 371 - 81, 461 - 68, 530 - 38. Illustrated. Juvenile.

The Lost Mountain: A Tale of Sonora. London: Routledge, 1885. First appeared as *The Gold Seekers Guide: or, The Lost Mountain*. New York: Beadle and Adams, 1882. This work is a revision of one chapter from Reid's translation of Louis de Bellemare's *Wood-Rangers*. Juvenile.

The Pierced Heart and Other Stories. London: J. & R. Maxwell, [1885]. Contents: "Pierced Heart," "Brother Against Brother," "Ghost, or Grizzly?" "The Spectre at the Gate," "Among the Mangroves," "The Iguana Hunter," "A Twelve Miles' Wade," "Christmas in a Shooting Box," "The Love Test," "Jarocho Life," "Among the Palmettos," "Riding in Rodeo," and "Captured by Confeds."

Trapped in a Tree and Other Stories: London: Miles (Charterhouse Series), [n.d., but after 1867 on evidence of contents which are the same as *Guerilla Chief* (*q.v.*), omitting "Guerilla Chief" and "Despard," and adding "Rosanna."]

No Quarter! 3 vols. London: Sonnenschein and Co., 1888.

Popular Adventure Tales. London: Simpkin [1890]. Illustrated. Anthology comprising *Young Voyageurs, Forest Exiles*, and *Bush Boys*. Juvenile.

Doubtful Works

The catalogue of the British Museum lists Charles Beach as a pseudonym for Mayne Reid.

BEACH, CHARLES. *Andrew Deverel: The History of an Adventure in New Guinea.* 2 vols. London: R. Bentley, 1863.

_____. *Lost Lenore: or, The Adventures of a Rolling Stone.* Edited by Captain Mayne Reid. 3 vols. London: Skeet, 1864.

_____. *Left to the World.* 3 vols. London: J. Maxwell, 1865.

_____. *Never: The Trials and Perilous Adventures of Frederick Lonsdale. An Autobiography.* London: Virtue & Co., 1868.

_____. *The Way to Win: A Story of Adventure Afloat and Ashore.* London: Lockwood & Co., 1869.

_____. *Pitzmaroon: or, The Magic Hammer.* Springfield, Mass.: Whitney and Adams, 1874. The copy held by Newberry Library is listed under Mayne Reid.

_____. *Waifs of the World: or, Adventures Afloat and Ashore.* London: F. Warne & Co., [1878].

Wild Life: or, Adventures on the Frontier. A Tale of the Early Days of the Texan Republic. New York: R. M. De Witt, [1859]. London: R. Bentley, 1873. Probably spurious. Composite work. Title story plagiarized from Charles Sealsfield's [Karl Anton Postl] *Cabin Book* (1841). Items written by Reid: (1) "Brothers and Sisters: A Parisian Sketch," (2) "The Last Adventure of a Coquette," (3) "A Husband's Ruse," (4) "The Wounded Guerilla: A Sketch of the Late Campaign," (5) "Scouting Near Vera Cruz," (6) "Mexican Jealousy."

Rangers and Regulators. New York: Carleton, 1870. Listed under Reid's name in *Uniform Trade List Annual* for 1874, but probably spurious.

SECONDARY SOURCES

All published biographical data on Reid has been based on one of two editions of Elizabeth Reid's biography (or on a combination of the biographies and *Men of the Time*). Nineteenth-century criticism (aside from cursory book reviews and obituary notices) is practically non-existent and twentieth-century scholarship has not corrected this. The following is a selective list; other sources are cited in the text and in the notes.

GASTON, EDWIN W., JR. *The Early Novel of the Southwest 1818 - 1918.* Albuquerque; Univ. of New Mexico Press, 1961. Contains synopsis of *Scalp Hunters* and brief discussion of the work from an historical and regional perspective.

GORDON, DUDLEY. "The First 'Western' Author." *New Mexico*, 35 (July 1957), 25 - 27, 66. Largely faulty biographical and bibliographical information, with a few original insights based on Reid's correspondence with Charles F. Lummis, *q.v.*

HODGINS, FRANCIS EDWARD, JR. *The Literary Emancipation of a Region: The Changing Image of the American West in Fiction.* Ann Arbor, Mich.: University Microfilms, 1957, pp. 125 - 42. Presents one of the few critical attempts to assess Reid's place in the literature through textual analysis rather than biographical fallacy.

HOLYOAKE, MALTUS QUESTELL. "Captain Mayne Reid: Soldier and Novelist." *Strand Magazine*, 2 (July 1891), 93 - 102. The first part of this article is a mere condensation of *Captain Mayne Reid.* "Part II—A Reminiscence" contains some Reid letters not available elsewhere and an account of Reid's friendship with Holyoake.

LUMMIS, CHARLES F. *Mesa, Cañon and Pueblo.* New York: Century Co., 1925, pp. 15 - 19. Appreciative criticism based on Reid's glowing treatment of the American West.

Men of the Time: Biographical Sketches of Eminent Living Characters. London: Kent, 1859, pp. 631 - 32. Rare contemporaneous biographical sketch, presumably supplied by Reid himself. The data does not correlate with Elizabeth Reid's information, thus causing further confusion regarding the accuracy of extant sources.

MEYER, ROY W. "The Western American Fiction of Mayne Reid." *Western American Literature*, 3 (Summer 1968), 115 - 32. A perceptive discussion of the major works with a Western setting. Although limited in scope, this is the best modern critical treatment of Reid to date.

OLLIVANT, CHARLES. "Mayne Reid." *Uses: A Monthly New Church Journal of Evolutionary Reform*, 3 (November 1898 - February 1899), 121 -23; 134 - 37; 150 - 53; 169 - 72; 4 (May 1899 - March 1900), 19 - 23; 39 - 42; 71 - 74; 100 - 04; 123 - 26; 135 - 38; 166 - 70; 186 - 89; 5 (June 1900 - March 1901), 24 - 27; 74 - 77; 105 - 08; 121 - 25; 137 -40; 177 - 80. Title varies; sometimes listed as "Mayne Reid: An Appreciation." Comprises the manuscript of Ollivant's projected "Life" of Mayne Reid which Ollivant effectively proves to have been plagiarized by Elizabeth Reid in his review of *Captain Mayne Reid* (pages 137 - 40 above). Unfortunately, even Ollivant, Reid's dedicated private secretary and personal friend, does not provide biographical material of a substantive nature.

REID, ELIZABETH. *Mayne Reid: A Memoir of His Life.* London: Ward & Downey, 1890. Essentially the aimless recollections of a fond widow interspersed with voluminous excerpts from Reid's correspondence and published writings.

————, AND CHARLES H. COE. *Captain Mayne Reid: His Life and Adventures.* London: Greening, 1900. A revised version of *Memoir*, deleting a good deal of the extraneous correspondence but still comprised mostly of reprints of Reid's own writings and of undated newspaper accounts of his life and works, interspersed with affectionate anecdotes. Heavily indebted to Ollivant, above.

STARRETT, VINCENT. "Mayne Reid: Yankee Soldier." In *The American Legion Reader*. Ed. Victor Lasky. New York: Hawthorne, 1953, pp. 48 - 53. A revision of "Moustache and Saber," below.

————. "Moustache and Saber." In *Bookman's Holiday*. New York: Random House, 1942, pp. 167 - 82. Biographical sketch largely based on Mrs. Reid.

————. "With Sword and Pen." In *Books Alive*. New York: Random House, 1940, pp. 99 - 120. Discusses Reid as a soldier-author in the tradition of Cervantes, Camoens, Raleigh, etc.

STEELE, JOAN DOROTHY. *The Image of America in the Novels of Mayne Reid: A Study of a Romantic Expatriate*. Ann Arbor, Mich.: University Microfilms, 1970. Doctoral dissertation drawing heavily upon unpublished holograph letters to establish new biographical data.

————. "Mayne Reid: A Revised Bibliography." *Bulletin of Bibliography*, 29, 3 (July - September 1972), 95 - 100. Supercedes all previous bibliographies. Some errors in the primary bibliography are corrected in the present volume. The secondary bibliography is complete except for two additional book reviews: "*Finger of Fate*," *Athenaeum*, Feb. 3, 1872, p. 144; and "*The Death Shot*," *Saturday Review*, June 7, 1873, pp. 760 - 61.

STEWART HUNTER, J. V. B. "Captain of Romance." *Book Handbook* [London], (1950), pp. 455 - 68. A well-written précis of *Captain Mayne Reid*. Illustrations from Reid novels. Incomplete bibliography.

Index

(The works of Reid are listed under his name)

148